Edited by Natasha Fried & Lena Tabori

Design by Jon Glick

The Little Big Book of Life

welcome
BOOKS
New York • San Francisco

Published in 2011 by Welcome Books®
An imprint of Welcome Enterprises, Inc.
6 West 18 Street, New York, NY 10011
Tel (212) 989-3200; Fax (212) 989-3205
www.welcomebooks.com

Publisher: Lena Tabori
Project Director: Natasha Tabori Fried
Designer: Jon Glick
Activities: Sara Baysinger
Original line arts for comedic essays and feng shui map: Kate Shaw
Editorial assistants: Lawrence Chesler, Rebecca T. Gross, Nicholas Lui

ISBN: 978-1-59962-099-2

Original edition published by Welcome Books® in 2003
The Library of Congress has cataloged the original edition as follows:

The little big book of life: lessons, wisdom, humor, instructions & advice/edited by Natasha Tabori Fried
and Lena Tabori.
　　　　p. cm. – (Little big book series ; 15th)
　　　　ISBN: 0-941807-82-7

　　　　1. Life—Literary collections. 2. Conduct of life—Literary collections. I. Fried, Natasha. II.
Tabori, Lena. III Little big book (New York, N.Y.) ; 15.

PN6071.L6 L58 2003

　　　2002193355

First Edition
10 9 8 7 6 5 4 3 2 1
Printed in China

TABLE OF CONTENTS

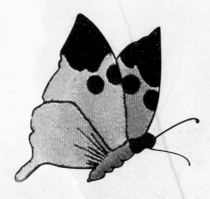

POETRY

SONGS

INTRODUCTION

"Hang on to your hat. Hang on to your hope.
And wind the clock, for tomorrow is another day."
E.B. White to Mr. Nadeau, March 30, 1973

I WAS IN A LITTLE SHOP IN KAUAI two years ago and found myself drawn to a small Buddha. I am not Buddist. But he was magic. He was dancing, and underneath him was written "joyful abandon." I took him home, and now he sits atop my kitchen stove. I am a cautious person, not prone to spontaneity. But "joyful abandon" is what I aspire to. And having that Buddha reminds me to relax, enjoy myself, and dream a little.

This image of Humpty Dumpty also comes from home. I meant it for the cover. And many agreed, until they remembered he fell off the wall, and "all the King's horses and all the King's men couldn't put Humpty Dumpty back together again." Then they found him depressing. But I still think Humpty is the perfect symbol. Look at him here: content, and somewhat Buddha-like, actually. And to me, that is the point of life: To stay balanced on the wall—to be happy.

There are many pieces here that are talismen for me. I carry a copy of Edgar Lee Master's *George Gray* in my checkbook. My grandmother taught me Robert Frost's *Road Less Traveled* when I was 8, along with the portion of Walt Whitman's *Leaves of Grass* reprinted here. *Desiderata* has been my Christmas card. The E.B. White quote above is pasted to my computer. And *The Green Stream*—sent as a birthday greeting from a friend—hangs in my bedroom.

But there is so much more, as I discovered researching this book. I fell in love with Ken Burns' speech to graduates at Hampshire college, F. Scott Fitzgerald's letter to his daughter, and Robert Fulgham's *All I Really Needed to Know I Learned in Kindergarten*. And the more humorous takes on life are so much fun: Kurt Vonnegut's answer to the secret of life (protein); and Ellen DeGeneres' suggested daily affirmations ("I mean for my hair to look like this.").

Enjoy. And be happy.

Natasha Fried

*Today is the first day
of the rest of your life.*

ABBIE HOFFMAN

Dreams

BY LANGSTON HUGHES

Hold fast to dreams

For if dreams die

Life is a broken-winged bird

That cannot fly.

Hold fast to dreams

For when dreams go

Life is a barren field

Frozen with snow.

from HITCHHIKER'S GUIDE TO THE GALAXY

BY DOUGLAS ADAMS

"WE'RE TRAPPED now, aren't we?"

"Yes," said Ford, "we're trapped."

"Well, didn't you think of anything? I thought you said you were going to think of something. Perhaps you thought of something and I didn't notice."

"Oh yes, I thought of something," panted Ford.

Arthur looked up expectantly.

"But unfortunately," continued Ford, "it rather involved being on the other side of this airtight hatchway." He kicked the hatch they'd just been thrown through.

"But it was a good idea, was it?"

"Oh yes, very neat."

"What was it?"

"Well, I hadn't worked out the details yet. Not much point now, is there?"

"So...er, what happens next?" asked Arthur.

"Oh, er, well, the hatchway in front of us will open automatically in a few moments and we will shoot out into deep space I expect and asphyxiate. If you take a lungful of air with you you can last for up to thirty seconds, of course…" said Ford. He stuck his hands behind his back, raised his eyebrows and started to hum an old Betelgeusian battle hymn. To Arthur's eyes he suddenly looked very alien.

"So this is it," said Arthur, "we are going to die."

"Yes," said Ford, "except…no! Wait a minute!" He suddenly lunged across the chamber at something behind Arthur's line of vision. "What's this switch?" he cried.

"What? Where?" cried Arthur, twisting round.

"No, I was only fooling," said Ford, "we are going to die after all."

He slumped against the wall again and carried on the tune from where he left off.

"You know," said Arthur, "it's at times like this, when I'm trapped in a Vogon airlock with a man from Betelgeuse, and about to die of asphyxiation in deep space, that I really wish I'd listened to what my mother told me when I was young."

"Why, what did she tell you?"

"I don't know, I didn't listen."

HI! HOW ARE YA? You got your stuff with you? I'll bet you do. Guys have stuff in their pockets; women have stuff in their purses. Of course, some women have pockets, and some guys have purses. That's OK. There's all different ways of carryin' your stuff.

A Place for Your Stuff

BY GEORGE CARLIN

Then there's all the stuff you have in your car. You got stuff in the trunk. Lotta different stuff: spare tire, jack, tools, old blanket, extra pair of sneakers. Just in case you wind up barefoot on the highway some night.

And you've got other stuff in your car. In the glove box. Stuff you might need in a hurry: flashlight, map, sunglasses, automatic weapon. You know. Just in case you wind up barefoot on the highway some night.

So stuff is important. You gotta take care of your stuff. You gotta have a *place* for your stuff. Everybody's gotta have a place for their stuff. That's what life is all about, tryin' to find a place for your stuff! That's all your house is: a place to keep your stuff. If you didn't have so much stuff, you wouldn't *need* a house. You could just walk around all the time.

A house is just a pile of stuff with a cover on it. You can see that when you're taking off in an airplane. You look down and see all the little piles of stuff. Everybody's got his own little pile of stuff. And they lock it up! That's right! When you leave your house, you gotta lock it up. Wouldn't want somebody to come by and *take* some of your stuff. 'Cause they always take the *good* stuff! They don't bother with that crap you're saving. Ain't nobody interested in your fourth-grade arithmetic papers. *National Geographics*, commemorative plates, your prize collection of Navajo underwear; they're not interested. They just want the good stuff; the shiny stuff; the electronic stuff.

So when you get right down to it, your house is nothing more than a place to keep your stuff…while you go out and get…*more* stuff. 'Cause that's what this country is all about. Tryin' to get more stuff. Stuff you don't want, stuff you don't need, stuff that's poorly made, stuff that's overpriced. Even stuff you can't afford! Gotta keep on gettin' more stuff. Otherwise someone else might wind up with more stuff. Can't let that happen. Gotta have the most stuff.

So you keep gettin' more and more stuff, and puttin' it in different places. In the closets, in the attic, in the basement, in the garage. And there might even be some stuff you left at your parents' house: baseball cards, comic books, photographs, souvenirs. Actually, your parents threw that stuff out long ago.

So now you got a houseful of stuff. And, even though you might like your house, you gotta move. Gotta get a bigger house. Why? Too much stuff! And that means you gotta move all your stuff. Or maybe, put some of your stuff in storage. Storage! Imagine that. There's a whole industry based on keepin' an eye on other people's stuff.

Or maybe you could sell some of your stuff. Have a yard sale, have a garage sale! Some people drive around all weekend just lookin' for garage sales. They don't have enough of their own stuff, they wanna buy other people's stuff.

Or you could take your stuff to the swap meet, the flea market, the rummage sale, or the auction. There's a lotta ways to get rid of stuff. You can even give your stuff away. The Salvation Army and Goodwill will actually come to your house and pick up your stuff and give it to people who don't have much stuff. It's part of what economists call the Redistribution of Stuff.

OK, enough about your stuff. Let's talk about other people's stuff. Have you ever noticed when you visit someone else's house, you never quite feel at home? You know why? No room for your stuff! Somebody *else's* stuff is all over the place. And what crummy stuff it is! "God! Where'd they get *this* stuff?"

And you know how sometimes when you're visiting someone, you unexpectedly have to stay overnight? It gets real late, and you decide to stay over? So they put you in a bedroom they don't use too often…because Grandma died in it eleven years ago! And they haven't moved any of her stuff? Not even the vaporizer?

Or whatever room they put you in, there's usually a dresser or a nightstand, and there's never any room on it for your stuff. Someone else's shit is on the dresser! Have you noticed that their stuff is shit, and your shit is stuff? "Get this shit off of here, so I can put my stuff down!" Crap is also a form of stuff. Crap is the stuff that belongs to the person you just broke up with. "When are you comin' over here to pick up the rest of your crap?"

Now, let's talk about traveling. Sometimes you go on vacation, and you gotta take some of your stuff. Mostly stuff to wear. But which stuff should you take? Can't take all your stuff. Just the stuff you really like; the stuff that fits you well that month. In effect, on vacation, you take a smaller, "second version" of your stuff.

Let's say you go to Honolulu for two weeks. You gotta take two big suitcases of stuff. Two weeks, two big suitcases. That's the stuff you check onto the plane. But you also got your carry-on stuff, plus the stuff you bought in the airport. So now you're all set to go. You got stuff in the overhead rack, stuff under the seat, stuff in the seat pocket, and stuff in your lap. And let's not forget the stuff you're gonna steal from the airline: silverware, soap, blanket, toilet paper, salt and pepper shakers. Too bad those headsets won't work at home.

And so you fly to Honolulu, and you claim your stuff—if the airline didn't drop it in the ocean—and you go to the hotel, and the first thing you do is put away your stuff. There's lots of places in a hotel to put your stuff.

"I'll put some stuff in here, you put some stuff in there. Hey, don't put your stuff in *there*! That's my stuff! Here's another place! Put some stuff in here. And there's another place! Hey, you know what? We've got more places than we've got stuff! We're gonna hafta go out and buy…*more stuff*!!!"

Finally you put away all your stuff, but you don't quite feel at ease, because you're a long way from home. Still, you sense that you must be OK, because you do have some of your stuff with you. And so you relax in Honolulu on that basis. That's when your friend from Maui calls and says, "Hey, why don't you come over to Maui for the weekend and spend a couple of nights over here?"

Oh no! Now whaddya bring? Can't bring all this stuff. You gotta bring an even *smaller* version of your stuff. Just enough stuff for a weekend on Maui. The "third version" of your stuff.

And, as you're flyin' over to Maui, you realize that you're really spread out now: You've got stuff all over the world!! Stuff at home, stuff in the garage, stuff at your parents' house (maybe), stuff in storage, stuff in Honolulu, and stuff on the plane. Supply lines are getting longer and harder to maintain!

Finally you get to your friends' place on Maui, and they give you a little room to sleep in, and there's a nightstand. Not much room on it for your stuff, but it's OK because you don't have much stuff now. You got your 8 x 10 autographed picture of Drew Carey, a large can of gorgonzola-flavored Cheeze Whiz, a small, unopened packet of brown confetti, a relief map of Corsica, and a family-size jar of peppermint-flavored, petrified egg whites. And you know that even though you're a long way from home, you must be OK because you do have a good supply of peppermint-flavored, petrified egg whites. And so you begin to relax in Maui on that basis. That's when your friend says, "Hey, I think tonight we'll go over to the other side of the island and visit my sister. Maybe spend the night over there."

Oh no! Now whaddya bring? right! You gotta bring an even smaller version. The "fourth version" of your stuff. Just the stuff you know you're gonna need: Money, keys, comb, wallet, lighter, hankie, pen, cigarettes, contraceptives, Vaseline, whips, chains, whistles, dildos, and a book. Just the stuff you *hope* you're gonna need....

By the way, if you go to the beach while you're visiting the sister, you're gonna have to bring—that's right—an even smaller version of your stuff: the "fifth version." Cigarettes and wallet. That's it. You can always borrow someone's suntan lotion. And then suppose, while you're there on the beach, you decide to walk over to the refreshment stand to get a hot dog? That's right, my friend! Number six! The most important version of your stuff: your wallet! Your wallet contains the only stuff you really can't do without.

Well, by the time you get home you're pretty fed up with your stuff and all the problems it creates. And so about a week later, you clean out the closet, the attic, the basement, the garage, the storage locker, and all the other places you keep your stuff, and you get things down to manageable proportions. Just the right amount of stuff to lead a simple and uncomplicated life. And that's when the phone rings. It's a lawyer. It seems your aunt has died... and left you all her stuff. Oh no! Now whaddya do? Right. You do the only thing you can do. The honorable thing. You tell the lawyer to stuff it.

Become a possibilitarian.
No matter how dark things seem
to be or actually are, raise your
sights and see possibilities—always
see them, for they're always there.

NORMAN VINCENT PEALE

Both Sides Now

BY JONI MITCHELL

Bows and flows of angel hair,
And ice cream castles in the air,
And feather canyons ev'rywhere,
I've looked at clouds that way.

But now they only block the sun,
They rain and snow on everyone.
So many things I would have done,
But clouds got in my way.

I've looked at clouds from both sides now,
From up and down and still somehow
It's cloud illusions I recall:
I really don't know clouds at all.

Moons and Junes and ferris wheels,
The dizzy dancing way you feel,
As ev'ry fairy tale comes real,
I've looked at love that way.

But now it's just another show,
you leave'em laughing when you go,
And if you care, don't let them know,
Don't give yourself away.

I've looked at love from both sides now,
From give and take and still somehow
It's love's illusions I recall:
I really don't know love at all.

Tears and fears and feeling proud,
To say "I love you" right out loud.
Dreams and schemes and circus crowds.
I've looked at love that way.

But now old friends are acting strange,
They shake their heads, they say I've changed.
But something's lost but something's gained,
In living ev'ry day.

MAYA ANGELOU

OCTOBER, 1977

ONE OF THE FIRST THINGS that a young person must internalize, deep down in the blood and bones, is the understanding that although he may encounter many defeats, he must not be defeated. If life teaches us anything, it may be that it's necessary to suffer some defeats. Look at a diamond: It is the result of extreme pressure. Less pressure, it is crystal; less than that, it's coal; and less than that, it is fossilized leaves or just plain dirt. It's necessary, therefore, to be tough enough to bite the bullet as it is shot into one's mouth, to bite it and stop it before it tears a hole in one's throat. One must learn to care for oneself first, so that one can then dare to care for someone else. That's what it takes to make the caged bird sing.

So Much Happiness

BY NAOMI SHIHAB NYE

It is difficult to know what to do with
   so much happiness.
With sadness there is something to rub
   against,
a wound to tend with lotion and cloth.
When the world falls in around you,
   you have pieces to pick up,
something to hold in your hands,
   like ticket stubs or change.

But happiness floats.
It doesn't need you to hold it down.
It doesn't need anything.
Happiness lands on the roof
   of the next house, singing,
and disappears when it wants to.
You are happy either way.
Even the fact that you once lived
   in a peaceful tree house
and now live over a quarry of noise and dust

cannot make you unhappy.
Everything has a life of its own,
it too could wake up filled with possibilities
of coffee cake and ripe peaches,
and love even the floor which needs
   to be swept,
the soiled linens and scratched records....

Since there is no place large enough
to contain so much happiness,
you shrug, you raise your hands,
   and it flows out of you
into everything you touch. You are not
   responsible.
You take no credit, as the night sky
   takes no credit
for the moon, but continues to hold it, and
   share it,
and in that way, be known.

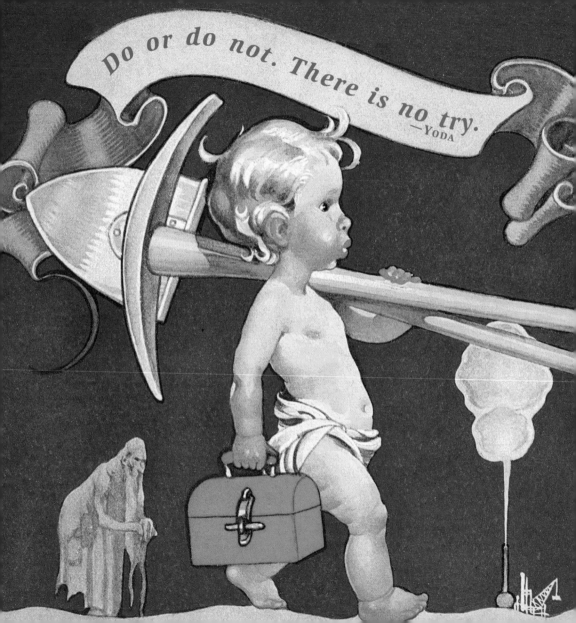

Do or do not. There is no try.
—YODA

A "TO DO" LIST FOR YOUR LIFE

A h, the "To Do" list—an unfortunate, but entirely necessary, feature of life. Mocking you with its outline of your failures, it can become a daily reminder of your inadequacy. (After all, what is worse than transferring old tasks to a fresh list?) On the other hand, it can inspire great productivity. Keeping you to task, a list can help you focus and build momentum. And, there is nothing like that blissful moment when you are finally able to cross off the last of your responsibilities.

Some busy days, it is the tool that prevents your head from falling off. Other days, it is a great distraction from the real tasks that lay ahead. Many people swear by it as the ultimate in organization tools. Others loathe turning their life's goals into a litany of tasks. If you are a member of this second group—the loathers—take heart. There is a list that you will love: The List!

The List contains all your daydreams and life wishes—it is your "fantastic imaginings" list. A list of this kind can be very empowering. It provides an opportunity for you to be selfish and focus on your wants, goals, and desires. Writing down your wish list can help you discover what it is you want out of life. Taking the time to articulate your goals increases the probability that you'll achieve them.

So take a break from your ordinary "to dos"—"do laundry; pay bills, schedule doctor appointment." Instead, find a block of time when you can sit in a cozy chair with your cup of coffee, grab a pen and paper (the nicer the better), and write "The List." Here are the rules:

Use a pen! A permanent wish list
provides the impetus for action.

The list cannot include a single mundane task.

The sky's the limit.

Don't let anyone else influence your list.

Mix attainable goals (learn to golf) in with your
most outrageous fantasies (walk on the moon!)

Include behavioral goals (quit smoking) among the more
task-oriented ones (assemble a photo album of your life.

Once you've written your list, put it in a safe, secret place. Don't drive yourself crazy looking at it everyday. Pull it out when the mood strikes you. It can help keep you grounded and provide some much-needed perspective during times of stress. Looking at your list after some time has elapsed can show you how you've evolved and if your goals have shifted.

HERE'S A SAMPLE LIST:
Master another language
Run a marathon
Complete the crossword puzzle (without using any reference materials!)

Learn an instrument
Blow bubbles
Write a book
Fall in love
Teach a child how to throw a ball
Attend an opera
Go skydiving
Build a sand castle
Learn to juggle
Go on Safari
Swim with dolphins
Read the bible
Win a Halloween costume contest
Invent something
Drive in London (safely!)
Cook a Thanksgiving dinner
Plant and tend a garden
Travel to the Great Pyramids
Skinny-dip
See your favorite musician in concert
Dance on a tabletop
Fly a kite
Scuba dive
Climb a mountain
Have a baby
Volunteer on a holiday

Try to remain humble.
Smartness kills everything.

SHERWOOD ANDERSON

George Gray

By Edgar Lee Masters

I have studied many times
The marble which was chiseled for me—
A boat with a furled sail at rest in a harbor.
In truth it pictures not my destination
But my life.
For love was offered me and I shrank from its disillusionment;
Sorrow knocked at my door, but I was afraid;
Ambition called to me, but I dreaded the chances.
Yet all the while I hungered for meaning in my life.
And now I know that we must lift the sail
And catch the winds of destiny
Wherever they drive the boat.
To put meaning in one's life may end in madness,
But life without meaning is the torture
Of restlessness and vague desire—
It is a boat longing for the sea and yet afraid.

AUTHOR JOHN STEINBECK TO HIS 14-YEAR-OLD SON, THOM

NOVEMBER 10, 1958

Dear Thom:

We had your letter this morning. I will answer it from my point of view and of course Elaine will from hers.

First—if you are in love—that's a good thing—that's about the best thing that can happen to anyone. Don't let anyone make it small or light to you.

Second—There are several kinds of love. One is a selfish, mean, grasping, egotistical thing which uses love for self-importance. This is the ugly and crippling kind. The other is an outpouring of everything good in you—of kindness, and consideration and respect—not only the social respect of manners but the greater respect which is recognition of another person as unique and valuable. The first kind can make you sick and small and weak but the second can release in you strength, and courage and goodness and even wisdom you didn't know you had.

You say this is not puppy love. If you feel so deeply—of course it isn't puppy love.

But I don't think you were asking me what you feel. You know that better than anyone. What you wanted me to help you with is what to do about it—and that I can tell you.

Glory in it for one thing and be very glad and grateful for it. The object of love is the best and most beautiful. Try to live up to it.

If you love someone—there is no possible harm in saying so—only you must remember that some people are very shy and sometimes the saying must take that shyness into consideration.

Girls have a way of knowing or feeling what you feel, but they usually like to hear it also.

It sometimes happens that what you feel is not returned for one reason or another—but that does not make your feeling less valuable and good.

Lastly, I know your feeling because I have it and I am glad you have it.

We will be glad to meet Susan. She will be very welcome. But Elaine will make all such arrangements because that is her province and she will be very glad to. She knows about love too and maybe she can give you more help than I can.

And don't worry about losing. If it is right, it happens—The main thing is not to hurry. Nothing good gets away.

Love

Fa

41

The Grand essentials to happiness in this life are something to do, something to love and something to hope for.

ECCLESIASTES 3:1–8

King James Bible

To every thing there is a season, and a time to
  every purpose under the heaven:
A time to be born, and a time to die; a time to plant,
  and a time to pluck up that which is planted;
A time to kill, and a time to heal; a time to break
  down, and a time to build up;
A time to weep, and a time to laugh; a time to mourn,
  and a time to dance;
A time to cast away stones, and a time to gather stones
  together; a time to embrace, and a time to refrain
  from embracing;
A time to get, and a time to lose; a time to keep, and a
  time to cast away;
A time to rend, and a time to sew; a time to keep
  silence, and a time to speak;
A time to love, and a time to hate; a time of war, and a
  time of peace.

GO PLACIDLY amid the noise and the haste, and remember what peace there may be in silence. As far as possible, without surrender, be on good terms with all persons. Speak your truth quietly and clearly; and listen to the dull and ignorant; they too have their story. Avoid loud and aggressive persons; they are vexations to the spirit. If you compare yourself with others, you may become vain or bitter, for always there will be greater and lesser persons than yourself. Enjoy your achievements as well as your plans. Keep interested in your career, however humble; it is a real possession in the changing fortunes of time. Exercise caution in your business affairs, for the world is full of trickery.

Desiderata
(something desired as essential)

MAX EHRMANN

But let this not blind you to what virtue there is; many persons strive for high ideals and everywhere life is full of heroism. Be yourself. Especially do not feign affection. Neither be cynical about love; for in the face of all aridity and disenchantment, it is as perennial as the grass. Take kindly the counsel of the years, gracefully surrendering the things of youth. Nurture strength of spirit to shield you in sudden misfortune. But do not distress yourself

with imaginings. Many fears are born of fatigue and loneliness. Beyond a wholesome discipline be gentle to yourself. You are a child of the universe, no less than the trees and the stars and you have a right to be here. And whether or not it is clear to you, no doubt the universe is unfolding as it should. Therefore, be at peace with God, whatever you conceive Him to be. And whatever your labors and aspirations, in the noisy confusion of life, keep peace with your soul. With all its sham, drudgery and broken dreams, it is still a beautiful world. Be cheerful. Strive to be happy.

Secret O' Life

WORDS AND MUSIC BY JAMES TAYLOR

The secret of life is enjoying
  the passage of time.
Any fool can do it.
There ain't nothing to it.
Nobody knows how we got
  to the top of the hill.
But since we're on our way down,
  we might as well enjoy the ride.

The secret of love is in
  opening up your heart.
It's OK to feel afraid.
But don't let that stand in your way.
'Cause anyone knows that love
  is the only road.
But since we're only here for awhile,
  might as well show some style.

The thing about time is that time isn't
  really real.
It's just your point of view.
How does it feel for you?
Einstein said he could never
  understand it all.
Planets spinning through space;
  the smile upon your face.

Give us a smile. Isn't it a lovely ride?
  Sliding down; gliding down.
Try not to try too hard.
  It's just a lovely ride.

Welcome to the human race.
Some kind of lovely ride.
I'll be sliding down; I'll be gliding down.
Try not to try too hard.
It's just a lovely ride.

Hope is a risk that must be run.

GEORGES BERNANOS

STEPHEN BREYER

STANFORD UNIVERSITY
JUNE 15, 1997

...THIS BRINGS ME TO A MORE DIFFICULT MATTER—a word of advice, as you try to decide "what next?" Your hearing what advantages your fine education has given you, while true, will not help you with those decisions. When I graduated, we received lots of advice: "Join the Army." "Give Blood." "Travel East." "Stay West." "The future is plastics." Have you seen *The Graduate*? There is always the risk that advice reflects the tunnel vision of one's own career. Supposedly someone asked Conrad Hilton what he might pass on to others after fifty years in the hotel business, and he replied, "Always keep the shower curtain inside the bathtub."

And of course you will be advised to ask many questions. In your careers the science graduate will ask, "Why does that work?"; the engineering graduate, "How does it work?"; the economics graduate, "What does it cost?"; and the liberal arts graduate, "Do you want french fries with that hamburger?"

But some advice rings true. Bayless Manning, former dean of Stanford Law School, pointed out to me once that when we make an important personal decision, we rarely know more than 10 percent of all we would like to know about it, let alone about the other options that the decision precludes.

Sometimes agonizing does not help; sometimes we must simply choose. And our lives then shape themselves around the choices that we make.

I take to heart an essay I once read about *Jane Eyre*. We look out, says the essayist, over any large city, and we are tempted to think that the lives within it are depressingly similar; but Charlotte Brontë's story of a governess reminds us that that is not so. It tells us that every person's life is a story of passion, with its moments of joy and happiness, of tragedy or sorrow. And each person's story is different, one from the other.

The external circumstances, the material circumstances, of that story are often beyond our control, but they often matter less than we think. We all know many people who complain despite having a glass full to overflowing. And my wife, who works with children at Dana Farber Cancer Institute, sees many families who bring joy to others and to themselves by seeing a glass half full that others see half empty.

The most important parts of the story are the personal parts as, through our choices, we create the story. Your story will include friends and family, not just career. And at times it will call upon you to participate in the life of the community in which you live and to help those who are less fortunate.

Most important, our stories include our own justifications for our actions and our motives—in light of our own values. We cannot escape the negative meaning that a failure of integrity—a failure to live up to our own basic standards of right and wrong—will give to the story that throughout our lives we tell ourselves. I agree with the philosopher who said that money can vanish overnight, power disappear, even that bubble reputation can evaporate, but character—personal integrity—is a rock that is secure and that no one can take from you....

The Road Not Taken

BY ROBERT FROST

Two roads diverged in a yellow wood,
And sorry I could not travel both
And be one traveler, long I stood
And looked down one as far as I could
To where it bent in the undergrowth;

Then took the other, as just as fair,
And having perhaps the better claim,
Because it was grassy and wanted wear;
Though as for that the passing there
Had worn them really about the same,

And both that morning equally lay
In leaves no step had trodden black.
Oh, I kept the first for another day!
Yet knowing how way leads on to way,
I doubted if I should ever come back.

I shall be telling this with a sigh
Somewhere ages and ages hence:
Two roads diverged in a wood, and I—
I took the one less traveled by,
And that has made all the difference.

THE SCENIC ROUTE

Life is what happens when you're busy
making other plans. —John Lennon

So often in life, memories and rich experiences are not the result of a well-laid plan, but rather a detour. If you are always planning things to the letter, you never leave room for surprises. So follow your whims and spontaneous impulses. Deviating from your norm can be lots of fun!

TEST YOUR PROPENSITY FOR SPONTANEITY.

WHEN YOU ARE TRAVELING

    a) You always have every reservation made in advance.

    b) You have reservations lined up for some nights, and not others.

    c) You wing it entirely. Your only safety net is the tent and sleeping bag in your trunk.

AT A PARTY

    a) You always stay in your comfort zone of close friends.

    b) You make an effort to meet a few new people, but always need to have your best friend by your side.

    c) You try to meet as many new people as possible, and ignore your friends.

ON A ROAD TRIP

a) You map out the whole trip to be as quick and efficient as possible.

b) You look at the map along the way and try to take as many scenic routes as time allows.

c) Map? What map?

WHEN YOU COOK

a) You always repeat dishes you know.

b) You discover new recipes to follow all the time.

c) You invent new dishes all the time, and rarely consult a cookbook.

WHEN YOU GO OUT TO EAT

a) You always go to the same restaurant and order the same dish.

b) You explore different restaurants in your neighborhood and settle on a couple.

c) You try a new restaurant whenever possible and tell the waiter to bring you their favorite dishes.

Give yourself 2 points for each time you answered (a); 5 points for each (b); and 10 points for each (c).

10-19 Predictability isn't all it's cracked up to be. Get out and live a little!
20-39 You really know how to live the good life! Keep it up!
40-50 Unless you like sleeping by the side of the road, getting lost, having mediocre meals, etc., you probably need to rein yourself in a little.

As you walk and eat and travel, be where you are. Otherwise you will miss most of your life.

BUDDHA

JESSIE WILLCOX SMITH.

Story for Margarita

BY RUBÉN DARÍO

Margarita the sea is gleaming
and the breeze
brings the scent of lemon
and orange sprays,
and in my soul I feel a lark singing:
your voice.

Margarita, I'm going to tell you
a story.

Once there was a king who had
a herd of elephants,
a tent made of daylight,
a palace of diamonds,

a kiosk of malachite,
a robe of gold tissue
and a graceful daughter

so lovely,
Margarita,
as lovely as you.

One afternoon the princess
looked up, and a new star shone.
She was mischievous,
and craved to get it down.

She wanted it for her breastpin,
to add to its décor,
with a poem and a pearl,
a feather and a flower.

Exquisite princesses
act a lot like you:
they cut roses and irises
and stars. Just like you.

So she went, the beautiful child,
under the sky and over the sea
to cut down the small white star
that had made her sigh.

She made her way upward
past the moon and farther;
with mischief, without permission
from her father.

When she left God's park
and returned that night,
she saw everything caught
in sweet, elegant light.

The king asked, "What have you done?
I looked all over—but you were lost!
And why are you blushing?
What's hiding there at your chest?"

The princess didn't lie.
What she told the king was true:
"I went to cut my star
out of the giant blue."

The king cried, "Haven't I told you
the blue is not to be touched?
What foolishness! What fancy!
Child, you'll anger God!"

She said, "I didn't mean to.
I don't know why I went
to the star, to cut it down.
I rode on the waves and the wind."

Her father, angry now, said:
"You must go back to heaven.
Your punishment is to return
what you have stolen."

The princess felt deeply sad—
her precious flower of light!
Then the good Lord appeared,
smiling, at her side.

He said, "From my far fields,
I offer this rose—to keep.
Stars are the flowers of children
who dream of me when they sleep."

The king dressed in brilliant robes
and in a procession he
marched four hundred elephants
down to the shore of the sea.

The princess is beautiful—
and she still wears the star in the pin
that the poem, pearl, feather
and flower shine in.

Margarita, the sea is gleaming
and the breeze
brings the scent of lemon
and orange sprays:
your breath.

Child, now that you'll be far,
remember the princess and the star.

And remember the one
who told you a story.

AUTHOR F. SCOTT FITZGERALD TO HIS DAUGHTER "PIE"

AUGUST 8, 1933

Dear Pie:

I feel very strongly about you doing [your] duty. Would you give me a little more documentation about your reading in French? I am glad you are happy—but I never believe much in happiness. I never believe in misery either. Those are things you see on the stage or the screen or the printed page, they never really happen to you in life.

All I believe in in life is the rewards for virtue (according to your talents) and the PUNISHMENTS for not fulfilling your duties, which are doubly costly. If there is such a volume in the camp library, will you ask Mrs. Tyson to let you look up a sonnet of Shakespeare's in which the line occurs "LILIES THAT FESTER SMELL WORSE THAN WEEDS."

Have had no thoughts today, life seems composed of getting up a SATURDAY EVENING POST story. I think of you, and always pleasantly; but if you call me "Pappy" again I am going to take the White Cat out and BEAT HIS BOTTOM HARD, SIX TIMES FOR EVERY TIME YOU ARE IMPERTINENT. Do you react to that?

I will arrange the camp bill.

Halfwit, I will conclude.

THINGS TO WORRY ABOUT:
    Worry about courage
    Worry about cleanliness
    Worry about efficiency
    Worry about horsemanship
    Worry about . . .

THINGS NOT TO WORRY ABOUT:
    Don't worry about popular opinion
    Don't worry about dolls
    Don't worry about the past
    Don't worry about the future
    Don't worry about growing up
    Don't worry about anybody getting ahead of you
    Don't worry about triumph
    Don't worry about failure unless it comes through your own fault
    Don't worry about mosquitos
    Don't worry about flies

Don't worry about insects in general
Don't worry about parents
Don't worry about boys
Don't worry about disappointments
Don't worry about pleasures
Don't worry about satisfactions

THINGS TO THINK ABOUT:
What am I really aiming at?
How good am I really in comparison to my
contemporaries in regard to:
    (a) Scholarship
    (b) Do I really understand about people
        and am I able to get along with them?
    (c) Am I trying to make my body a useful
        instrument or am I neglecting it?

               With dearest love,
               Daddy

*If A is success in life,
then A equals X plus Y plus Z.
Work is X, Y is play, and Z
is keeping your mouth shut.*

ALBERT EINSTEIN

from CATCH 22

Joseph Heller

DUNBAR LOVED SHOOTING SKEET because he hated every minute of it and the time passed so slowly. He had figured out that a single hour on the skeet-shooting range with people like Havermeyer and Appleby could be worth as much as eleven-times-seventeen years.

"I think you're crazy," was the way Clevinger had responded to Dunbar's discovery.

"Who wants to know?" Dunbar answered.

"I mean it," Clevinger insisted.

"Who cares?" Dunbar answered.

"I really do. I'll even go so far as to concede that life seems longer i—"

"—*is* longer i—"

"—*is* longer—*Is* longer? All right, *is* longer if it's filled with periods of boredom and discomfort, b—"

"Guess how fast?" Dunbar said suddenly.

"Huh?"

"They go," Dunbar explained.

"Who?"

"Years."

"Years?"

"Years," said Dunbar. "Years, years, years."

"Clevinger, why don't you let Dunbar alone?" Yossarian broke in. "Don't you realize the toll this is taking?"

"It's all right," said Dunbar magnanimously. "I have some decades to spare. Do you know how long a year takes when it's going away?"

"And you shut up also," Yossarian told Orr, who had begun to snigger.

"I was just thinking about that girl," Orr said. "That girl in Sicily. That girl in Sicily with the bald head."

"You'd *better* shut up also," Yossarian warned him.

"It's your fault," Dunbar said to Yossarian. "Why don't you let him snigger if he wants to? It's better than having him talking."

"All right. Go ahead and snigger if you want to."

"Do you know how long a year takes when it's going away?" Dunbar repeated to Clevinger. "This long." He snapped his fingers.

"A second ago you were stepping into college with your lungs full of fresh air. Today you're an old man."

"Old?" asked Clevinger with surprise. "What are you talking about?"

"Old."

"I'm not old."

"You're inches away from death every time you go on a mission. How much older can you be at your age? A half minute before that you were stepping into high school, and an unhooked brassiere was as close as you ever hoped to get to Paradise. Only a fifth of a second before that you were a small kid with a ten-week summer vacation that lasted a hundred thousand years and still ended too soon. Zip! They go rocketing by so fast. How the hell else are you ever going to slow time down?" Dunbar was almost angry when he finished.

"Well, maybe it is true," Clevinger conceded unwillingly in a subdued tone. "Maybe a long life does have to be filled with many unpleasant conditions if it's to seem long. But in that event, who wants one?"

"I do," Dunbar told him.

"Why?" Clevinger asked.

"What else is there?"

WHEN YOUR LIFE GETS TO BE overwhelming, when you feel like too much of the world is depressing, there are two things you can do: One, sit in your house and feel the doom and gloom and continue to watch the news, shaking your head in resignation and saying to yourself, "Oh no, my life sucks. The world is ending, there's nothing I can do." This is one way to go. I, personally, wouldn't recommend it.

"Well," you say, "what's the *other* option?"

Daily Affirmations
or a cup of pudding a day is the way to stay o.k.

BY ELLEN DEGENERES

Here it is: If you must watch the news, turn the sound off and imagine the news anchor people are telling you all about your day. Make up happy events, adding your name into the report every third or fourth sentence.

Sing aloud with wild abandonment as you get dressed in the morning (any cheery song will do).

And most important, get yourself some daily affirmations.

I do daily affirmations every day—hence the word "daily." I guess, if you're lazy, you can do weekly affirmations or monthly affirmations or even yearly affirmations. Actually, I suppose New Year's resolutions are yearly affirmations.

But if you're making the same New Year's resolution every year (e.g., "I will be more popular"), and it's still not happening (e.g., "Nobody ever calls me. I'm all alone. Boo hoo."), it may be time to change your strategy. Your next yearly affirmation should be to do daily affirmations.

Daily affirmations are an important way to pick yourself up. We all have bad days and you can't always count on other people to make things better. For instance, you might say to someone, "I'm a bad person," expecting them to say in return, "Oh, no, you're not, you're one of the kindest, most thoughtful people I know." But nine times out of ten, they'll say instead, "Really. Hmmm. Hey, could you pass the Chee-tos?" And sometimes you're not even eating Chee-tos, you're eating barbecue potato chips or some weird flavored popcorn!

So, because you can't rely on other people, for your own ego you need daily affirmations. Some obvious affirmations are: "I am a good person" or "I love myself" or "I matter." But I think it's a good idea to start small. You should say things that make you feel good because they are easy to accomplish. ("I will wake up." "I will brush my teeth.") Don't push yourself. Those can be very good morning affirmations. I guess, though, if you're really depressed, and it's 8 o'clock at night, "I will wake up" would technically be an evening affirmation.

The more depressed you are, the simpler the affirmation should be. Under the right circumstances, "Who cares if I'm drunk?" is a perfectly reasonable affirmation.

Sometimes the only way you can make yourself feel better is by putting other people down. And that's okay. There is nothing wrong with that—whatever gets you through. "I'm not as fat as she is." "I have more teeth than he has." "Thank God I'm not as bone ugly as they are." These are all fine affirmations. However, it's best that when you're in public you say this kind of affirmation to yourself. It can save you embarrassment and a black eye. These are silent affirmations.

You probably do affirmations without even knowing it. Every time you drive over the speed limit, you're saying, "No copper is gonna catch me speeding." And when you put that ski mask over your head, you're saying, "Nobody is going to recognize me while I rob this gas station." You're pumping yourself up and telling yourself you can succeed.

Here are some affirmations that have helped me. Use them if you'd like. They're yours free (except for what you paid for the book; if you borrowed this book from a friend or the library and you feel you should send me a few bucks, that's fine, too).

I AM THE WORLD'S TALLEST MIDGET.

I'M A LITTLE TEAPOT, SHORT AND STOUT.
HERE IS MY HANDLE, HERE IS MY SPOUT.

I BET NOBODY KNOWS I'M CRAZY.

I LOOK GOOD IN BELL BOTTOMS.

ARCHIE WOULD RATHER DATE ME THAN EITHER BETTY OR VERONICA.

I CAN WALK THROUGH WALLS. OUCH! NO, I CAN'T.

I MEAN FOR MY HAIR TO LOOK LIKE THIS.

THE GREAT SPIRIT SMILES ON ME. ON ME AND ONLY ME.
THE GREAT SPIRIT HATES EVERYBODY ELSE. WE'RE BEST FRIENDS.

I DON'T NEED TO EXERCISE. I HAVE THE PERFECT SHAPE.

I'M SMARTER THAN MY DOGS. WELL, SMARTER THAN ONE OF MY DOGS.

I LOOK GOOD WITH BACK HAIR.
BEING GRUBBY EQUALS BEING COOL.

I SING BETTER THAN BONNIE RAITT. I HAVE AS MANY GRAMMYS AS BONNIE RAITT. I AM BONNIE RAITT.

IT'S NOT IMPORTANT TO KNOW WHAT EVERYBODY ELSE SEEMS TO KNOW. I DON'T CARE HOW MUCH THEY LAUGH AT ME.

LA LA LA LA LA LA LA LA LA LA LA LA—TALK ALL YOU WANT, I CAN'T HEAR YOU—LA LA LA LA LA LA LA LA. LA LA LA.

IF I PUT MY MIND TO IT, I COULD DO ANYTHING. I JUST DON'T FEEL LIKE PUTTING MY MIND TO SOMETHING. SO THERE.

I HAVE X-RAY VISION. WAIT A MINUTE. I DON'T. THESE GLASSES ARE A RIP-OFF.

I MEANT TO GET RIPPED OFF.

I'VE FALLEN AND I CAN GET UP.

I'M GOOD AT WATCHING TV.

I CAN COME UP WITH BETTER AFFIRMATIONS THAN THESE.

SMILE

WORDS BY JOHN TURNER AND GEOFFREY PARSONS

Smile, though your heart is aching
Smile, even though it's breaking
When there are clouds
In the sky, you'll get by if you
Smile through your pain and sorrow
Smile and maybe tomorrow
You'll see the sun
come shining through for you

Light up your face with gladness
Hide every trace of sadness
Although a tear may be ever so near
That's the time you must keep on trying
Smile, what's the use of crying
You'll find that life is still worthwhile
If you'll just smile

You will do foolish things,
but do them with enthusiasm.

COLETTE

RUSSELL BAKER

CONNECTICUT COLLEGE
MAY 27, 1995

…OVER THE YEARS I spoke to many graduating classes, always pleading with them: Whatever you do, do not go forth. Nobody listened. They kept right on going forth, and look what we have today…. So I will not waste my breath today pleading with you not to go forth. Instead I will limit myself to a simple plea: When you get out there in the world, try not to make it worse than it already is.

I thought it might help to give you a list of the hundred most important things you can do to avoid making the world any worse. Since I am shooting for fifteen minutes, however, you will have to make do with ten. Short as the public attention span is these days nobody could remember a hundred anyhow. Even ten may be asking too much.

You remember the old joke about how television news would have reported the Ten Commandments: "God today issued ten commandments, three of which are . . ." Here is my list, ten things to help you avoid making the world worse than it already is.

One, bend down and smell a flower.

Two, don't go around in clothes that talk. There is already too much talk in the world. We've got so many people talking there's hardly anybody left to listen. With radio and television and telephones we've got talking furniture; with bumper stickers we've got talking cars. Talking clothes just add to the uproar. If you simply cannot resist being an incompetent klutz, don't boast about it by wearing a T-shirt that says UNDERACHIEVER AND PROUD OF IT. Being dumb is not the worst thing in the world, but letting your clothes shout it out loud

depresses the neighbors and embar-
rasses your parents.

Point three follows from point two, and it's this: Listen once in a while. It's amazing what you can hear. On a hot summer day in the country you can hear the corn growing, the crack of a roof buckling under the power of the sun. In a real old-fashioned parlor, silence so deep you can hear the dust settling on the velveteen settee. You might hear the footsteps of something sinister gaining on you. Or a heart-stopping beautiful phrase from Mozart you haven't heard since childhood, or the voice of somebody— now gone—whom you loved. Or sometime when you're talking up a storm so brilliant, so charming you can hardly believe how wonderful you are, pause just a moment and listen to yourself. It's good for the soul to hear yourself as others hear you. And next time, maybe, just maybe, you will not talk so much, so loudly, so brilliantly, so charmingly, so utterly shamefully foolishly.

Point four, sleep in the nude. In an age when people don't even get dressed up to go to the theater, it's silly getting dressed up to go to bed. What's more, now that you can no longer smoke, drink, or eat bacon and eggs without somebody trying to make you feel ashamed of yourself, sleeping in the nude is one deliciously sinful pleasure you can commit without being caught by the Puritan squads that patrol the nation.

Point five: Turn off the TV once or twice a month and pick up a book. It will ease your blood pressure. It might even wake up your mind. But if it puts you to sleep, you're still a winner. Better to sleep than have to watch the endless parade of body bags the local news channel marches through your parlor.

Six, don't take your gun to town. Don't even leave it home unless you lock all your bullets in a safe-deposit box in a faraway bank. The surest way to get shot, contrary to popular impression, is not to drop by the near-est convenience store for a bottle of milk at midnight, but to keep a loaded pistol in your own house. What about your constitutional right to bear arms, you say? I would simply point out that you don't have to exercise a constitutional right just because you have it. You have the constitutional right to run for President of the United States, but most people have too much sense to insist on exercising it.

Seven, learn to fear the automobile. It's not the trillion-dollar deficit that will finally destroy America; it is the automobile. Congressional studies of future highway needs are terrifying. A typical projection shows that when your generation is middle-aged, Interstate 95 between Miami and Fort Lauderdale will have to be twenty-two lanes wide to avoid total paralysis of South Florida. Imagine an entire country covered with asphalt. My grandfather's generation shot horses. Yours had better learn to shoot automobiles.

Eight, have some children. Children add texture to your life. They will save you from becoming old fogies before you're middle-aged. They will teach you humility. When old age overtakes you, as it inevitably will, I'm sorry to say, having a few children will provide you with people who will feel guilty when being accused of being ungrateful for all you've done for them. It's almost impossible nowadays to find anybody who will feel guilty about anything, including mass murder. When you reach the golden years, your best bet is children, the ingrates.

Nine, get married. I know you don't want to hear this, but getting married will give you a lot more satisfaction in the long run than your BMW. It provides a standard set of parents for your children and gives you that second income you will need when it comes time to send those children to Connecticut College. What's more, without marriage you will have practically no material at all to work with when you decide to write a book, or hire a psychiatrist.

When you get married, whatever you do, do not ask a lawyer to draw up a marriage contract spelling out how your lives will be divvied up when you get divorced. It's hard enough to make a marriage work without having a blueprint for its destruction drawn up before you go to the altar. Speaking of lawyers brings me to point nine and a half, which is: Avoid lawyers unless you have nothing to do with the rest of your life but kill time.

And finally, point ten: Smile. You're one of the luckiest people in the world. You're living in America. Enjoy it. I feel obliged to give you this banal advice because although I've lived through the Great Depression, World War II, terrible wars in Korea and Vietnam, and a half-century of Cold War, I have never seen a time when there were so many Americans so angry or so meanspirited or so sour about the country as there are today. Anger has become the national habit. You see it on the sullen faces of fashion models scowling out of

magazines. It pours out of the radio. Washington television hams snarl and shout at each other on television.

Ordinary people abuse politicians and their wives with shockingly coarse insults. Rudeness has become an acceptable way of announcing you are sick and tired of it all and you're not going to take it anymore. Vile speech is justified on the same ground and is inescapable. America is angry at the press. Angry at immigrants, angry at television, angry at traffic, angry at people who are well off and angry at people who are poor. Angry at blacks and angry at whites. The old are angry at the young; the young are angry at the old. Suburbs are angry at cities; cities are angry at the suburbs. Rustic America is angry at both whenever urban and suburban invaders threaten the rustic sense of having escaped from God's angry land. A complete catalog of the varieties of bile poisoning the American soul would fill a library. The question is: Why? Why has anger become the common response to the inevitable ups and downs of national life? The question is baffling not just because the American habit even in the worst of times has been mindless optimism, but also because there is so little for Americans to be angry about nowadays. We are the planet's undisputed superpower. For the first time in six years we enjoy something very much like real peace. We are by all odds the wealthiest nation on earth, though admittedly our vast treasure is not evenly shared.

Forgive me the geezer's sin of talking about "the bad old days," but the country is still full of people who remember when thirty-five dollars a week was considered a living wage for a whole family. People whine about being overtaxed, yet in the 1950s the top income tax rate was 91 percent, universal military service was the law of the land, and racial segregation was legally enforced in large parts of the country. So what explains the fury and dyspepsia? I suppose it's the famous American ignorance of history. People who know nothing of even the most recent past are easily gulled by slick operators who prosper by exploiting the ignorant. Among these rascals are our politicians. Politicians flourish by sowing discontent. They triumph by churning discontent into anger. Press, television, and radio also have a big financial stake in keeping the country boiling mad.

Good news, as you know, does not sell papers or keep millions glued to radios and TV screens. So when you're out there in the world, ladies and gentlemen, you're going to find yourself surrounded by shouting, red-in-the-face, stomping mad politicians, radio yakmeisters, and yes, sad to say, newspaper columnists telling you, "You never had it so bad," and otherwise trying to spoil your day.

When they come at you with that line, ladies and gentlemen, give them a wink and a smile and a good view of your departing back. And as you stroll away, bend down to smell a flower....

If you have built castles in the air, your work need not be lost; that is where they should be. Now put the foundations under them.

HENRY DAVID THOREAU

MEDITATION: EXERCISE FOR THE MIND

Thus it is our own mind
that should be established in all the Roots of the Good;
it is our own mind
that should be soaked by the rain of truth;
it is our own mind
that should be purified from all obstructive qualities;
it is our own mind
that should be made vigorous by energy.
—Buddhist Scripture

Try to relax your mind for one minute. Clear it of all thought. It seems like a simple-enough task. But for those of us who are card-carrying members of the Overachievers Club, those sixty seconds feel like an eternity. Our modern world's focus on efficiency and results has bred a society of overworked, stressed-out insomniacs. Fortunately, there is an antidote to this madness: meditation.

Meditation may not be for everyone. You may have built up a great deal of pride regarding your multitasking skills. If so, then perhaps you should skip to the next few pages. Or ask yourself: Is it really healthy to base your self-worth solely on how many tasks you can complete simultaneously? Think about it! Are you really saving time? Are you giving each task the attention it requires in order to be done well? Or are you someone who thrives on stress? Do you feel you need it in order to succeed?

The benefits of meditation are endless. It can

Relieve stress by unblocking negative energy stored in your body
Calm your mind
Aid with concentration
Allow you to live in the moment
Make you feel more centered
Help you to complete tasks more proficiently
Reduce insomnia
Normalize blood pressure
Reduce heart disease
Mitigate depression and anxiety
Help you better retain what you read, see, and hear

So how do you learn to meditate? What are the rules? Do you need to be a Buddhist to know what you're doing? Well, the fact is that anyone can meditate. You can take a class in yoga, t'ai chi, or Qigong. Or just reserve a special space in your home where you go each day for silent thought. Practice your breathing while you take a quiet walk in the park. Even your daily shower provides a period of time and a place to practice meditation. It is always a good idea to stretch before you begin any meditation. Stretching relaxes your mind and invigorates your senses to give you increased focus. Here are some ways to get you into a meditative "pose" or state of mind:

As instructed before, practice relaxing your mind for one minute. At first, this will feel impossible. When your mind starts to race, just breath deeply and concentrate on the exhalation and inhalation of your breath.

Think of a specific object for one minute (e.g., an apple) Now try not to think of the same object for a minute. Practice steering your mind toward one idea, and away from an idea.

Focus your mind and relax your body through breathing. Take nine deep breaths, slowing them down as you go.

For five minutes, practice keeping your mind in the present. Open your thoughts and notice everything around you. Anytime you find yourself thinking of something in the past or future, snap your fingers. This is your cue to come back into the moment.

Meditation takes some practice. In the beginning, you may find that your body quivers or tingles as you attempt to achieve an alert yet relaxed state. This reaction is called the "release phenomenon." As the accumulated stress in your body begins to break down, your muscles unclench and release tension. Not only is this unknotting completely normal, it means you're off to a good start!

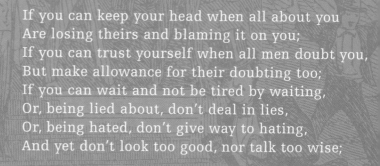

If

By Rudyard Kipling

If you can keep your head when all about you
Are losing theirs and blaming it on you;
If you can trust yourself when all men doubt you,
But make allowance for their doubting too;
If you can wait and not be tired by waiting,
Or, being lied about, don't deal in lies,
Or, being hated, don't give way to hating,
And yet don't look too good, nor talk too wise;

If you can dream—and not make dreams your maste
If you can think—and not make thoughts your aim;
If you can meet with triumph and disaster
And treat those two imposters just the same;
If you can bear to hear the truth you've spoken
Twisted by knaves to make a trap for fools,
Or watch the things you gave your life to broken,
And stoop and build 'em up with worn-out tools;

If you can make one heap of all your winnings
And risk it on one turn of pitch-and-toss,
And lose, and start again at your beginnings
And never breathe a word about your loss;
If you can force your heart and nerve and sinew
To serve your turn long after they are gone,
And so hold on when there is nothing in you
Except the Will which says to them: "Hold on";

If you can talk with crowds and keep your virtue,
Or walk with kings–nor lose the common touch;
If neither foes nor loving friends can hurt you;
If all men count with you, but none too much;
If you can fill the unforgiving minute
With sixty seconds' worth of distance run–
Yours is the Earth and everything that's in it,
And–which is more–you'll be a Man, my son!

WRITER JAMES BALDWIN TO HIS NEPHEW JAMES

ON THE 100TH ANNIVERSARY OF THE EMANCIPATION PROCLAMATION, 1963

Dear James:

....This innocent country set you down in a ghetto in which, in fact, it intended that you should perish. Let me spell out precisely what I mean by that, for the heart of the matter is here, and the root of my dispute with my country. You were born when you were born and faced the future that you faced because you were black and FOR NO OTHER REASON. The limits of your ambition were, thus, expected to be set forever. You were born into a society which spelled out with brutal clarity, and in as many ways as possible, that you were a worthless human being. You were not expected to aspire to excellence: you were expected to make peace with mediocrity. Wherever you have turned, James, in your short time on this earth, you have been told where you could go and what you could do (and HOW you could do it) and where you could live and whom you could marry. I know your countrymen do not agree with me about this, and I hear them saying, "You exaggerate." They do not know Harlem, and I do. So do you. Take no one's word for anything, including mine—but trust your experience. Know whence you came. If you know whence you came, there is really no limit to where you can go. The details and symbols of your life have been deliberately constructed to make you believe what white people say about you. Please try to remember what they believe, as well as what they do and cause you to endure, does not testify to your inferiority but to their humanity and fear. Please try to be clear, dear James, through the storm which rages about your youthful head today, about the reality which lies behind the words ACCEPTANCE and INTEGRATION. There is no reason for you to try to become like white people and there is no basis whatever for their impertinent assumption that THEY must accept YOU. The really terrible thing, old buddy, is that YOU must accept THEM. And I mean that very seriously. You must accept them and accept them with love. For these innocent people have no other hope.

They are, in effect, still trapped in a history which they do not understand; and until they understand it, they cannot be released from it. They have had to believe for many years, and for innumerable reasons, that black men are inferior to white men. Many of them, indeed, know better, but, as you will discover, people find it very difficult to act on what they know. To act is to be committed, and to be committed is to be in danger. In this case. the danger, in the minds of most white Americans, is the loss of their identity. Try to imagine how you would feel if you woke up one morning to find the sun shining and all the stars aflame. You would be frightened because it is out of the order of nature. Any upheaval in the universe is terrifying because it so profoundly attacks one's sense of one's own reality. Well, the black man has functioned in the white man's world as a fixed star, as an immovable pillar: and as he moves out of his place, heaven and earth are shaken to their foundations. You, don't be afraid. I said that it was intended that you should perish in the ghetto, perish by never being allowed to go behind the white man's definitions, by never being allowed to spell your proper name. You have, and many of us have, defeated this intention; and, by a terrible law, a terrible paradox, those innocents who believed that your imprisonment made them safe are losing their grasp of reality. But these young men are your brothers—your lost, younger brothers. And if the word INTEGRATION means anything, this is what it means: that we, with love, shall force our brothers to see themselves as they are, to cease fleeing from reality and begin to change it. For this is your home, my friend, do not be driven from it; great men have done great things here, and will again, and we can make America what America must become. It will be hard, James, but you come from sturdy, peasant stock, men who picked cotton and dammed rivers and built railroads, and, in the teeth of the most terrifying odds, achieved an unassailable and monumental dignity. You come from a long line of great poets, some of the greatest poets since Homer. One of them said, THE VERY TIME I THOUGHT I WAS LOST, MY DUNGEON SHOOK AND MY CHAINS FELL OFF....

Your uncle,
James

All you need in this life is ignorance and confidence, and then success is sure.

MARK TWAIN

INDIAN CAMP

By Ernest Hemingway

AT THE LAKE SHORE there was another rowboat drawn up.
The two Indians stood waiting.

Nick and his father got in the stern of the boat and the Indians
shoved it off and one of them got in to row. Uncle George sat in
the stern of the camp rowboat. The young Indian shoved the camp
boat off and got in to row Uncle George.

The two boats started off in the dark. Nick heard the oarlocks of
the other boat quite a way ahead of them in the mist. The Indians
rowed with quick choppy strokes. Nick lay back with his father's
arm around him. It was cold on the water. The Indian who was
rowing them was working very hard, but the other boat moved
further ahead in the mist all the time.

"Where are we going, Dad?" Nick asked.

"Over to the Indian camp. There is an Indian lady very sick."

"Oh," said Nick.

Across the bay they found the other boat beached. Uncle George
was smoking a cigar in the dark. The young Indian pulled the boat
way up on the beach. Uncle George gave both the Indians cigars.

INDIAN CAMP

They walked up from the beach through a meadow that was soaking wet with dew, following the young Indian who carried a lantern. Then they went into the woods and followed a trail that led to the logging road that ran back into the hills. It was much lighter on the logging road as the timber was cut away on both sides. The young Indian stopped and blew out his lantern and they all walked on along the road.

They came around a bend and a dog came out barking. Ahead were the lights of the shanties where the Indian bark-peelers lived. More dogs rushed out at them. The two Indians sent them back to the shanties. In the shanty nearest the road there was a light in the window. An old woman stood in the doorway holding a lamp.

Inside on a wooden bunk lay a young Indian woman. She had been trying to have her baby for two days. All the old women in the camp had been helping her. The men had moved off up the road to sit in the dark and smoke out of range of the noise she made. She screamed just as Nick and the two Indians followed his father and Uncle George into the shanty. She lay in the lower bunk, very big under a quilt. Her head was turned to one side. In the upper bunk was her husband. He had cut his foot very badly with an ax three days before. He was smoking a pipe. The room smelled very bad.

Nick's father ordered some water to be put on the stove, and while it was heating he spoke to Nick.

"This lady is going to have a baby, Nick," he said.

"I know," said Nick.

"You don't know," said his father. "Listen to me. What she is going through is called being in labor. The baby wants to be born and she wants it to be born. All her muscles are trying to get the baby born. That is what is happening when she screams."

"I see," Nick said.

Just then the woman cried out.

"Oh, Daddy, can't you give her something to make her stop screaming?" asked Nick.

"No. I haven't any anaesthetic," his father said. "But her screams are not important. I don't hear them because they are not important."

The husband in the upper bunk rolled over against the wall.

The woman in the kitchen motioned to the doctor that the water was hot. Nick's father went into the kitchen and poured about half of the water out of the big kettle into a basin. Into the water left in the kettle he put several things he unwrapped from a handkerchief.

"Those must boil," he said, and began to scrub his hands in the basin of hot water with a cake of soap he had brought from the camp. Nick watched his father's hands scrubbing each other with the soap. While his father washed his hands very carefully and thoroughly, he talked.

"You see, Nick, babies are supposed to be born head first but sometimes they're not. When they're not they make a lot of trouble for everybody. Maybe I'll have to operate on this lady. We'll know in a little while."

When he was satisfied with his hands he went in and went to work.

"Pull back that quilt, will you, George?" he said. "I'd rather not tough it."

Later when he started to operate Uncle George and three Indian men held the woman still. She bit Uncle George on the arm and Uncle George said, "damn squaw bitch!" and the young Indian who had rowed Uncle George over laughed at him. Nick held the basin for his father. It all took a long time. His father picked the baby up and slapped it to make it breathe and handed it to the old woman.

"See, it's a boy, Nick," he said. "How do you like being an interne?"

Nick said, "All right." He was looking away so as not to see what his father was doing.

"There. That gets it," said his father and put something into the basin. Nick didn't look at it.

"Now," his father said, "there's some stitches to put in. You can watch this or not, Nick, just as you like. I'm going to sew up the incision I made."

Nick did not watch. His curiosity had been gone for a long time.

His father finished and stood up. Uncle George and the three Indian men stood up. Nick put the basin out in the kitchen.

Uncle George looked at his arm. The young Indian smiled reminiscently.

"I'll put some peroxide on that, George," the doctor said. He bent over the Indian woman. She was quiet now and her eyes were closed. She looked very pale. She did not know what had become of the baby or anything.

"I'll be back in the morning," the doctor said, standing up. "The nurse should be here from St. Ignace by noon and she'll bring everything we need."

He was feeling exalted and talkative as football players are in the dressing room after a game.

"That's one for the medical journal, George," he said. "Doing a Caesarian with a jack-knife and sewing it up with nine-foot, tapered gut leaders."

INDIAN CAMP

Uncle George was standing against the wall, looking at his arm.

"Oh, you're a great man, all right," he said.

"Ought to have a look at the proud father. They're usually the worst sufferers in these little affairs," the doctor said. "I must say he took it all pretty quietly."

He pulled back the blanket from the Indian's head. His hand came away wet. He mounted on the edge of the lower bunk with the lamp in one hand and looked in. The Indian lay with his face toward the wall. His throat had been cut from ear to ear. The blood had flowed down into a pool where his body sagged the bunk. His head rested on his left arm. The open razor lay, edge up, in the blankets.

"Take Nick out of the shanty, George," the doctor said.

There was no need of that. Nick, standing in the door of the kitchen, had a good view of the upper bunk when his father, the lamp in one hand, tipped the Indian's head back.

It was just beginning to be daylight when they walked along the logging road back toward the lake.

"I'm terribly sorry I brought you along, Nickie," said his father, all his post-operative exhilaration gone. "It was an awful mess to put you through."

"Do ladies always have such a hard time having babies?" Nick asked.

"No, that was very, very exceptional."

"Why did he kill himself, Daddy?"

"I don't know, Nick. He couldn't stand things, I guess."

"Do many men kill themselves, Daddy?"

"Not very many, Nick."

"Do many women?"

"Hardly ever."

"Don't they ever?"

"Oh, yes. They do sometimes."

"Daddy?"

"Yes."

"Where did Uncle George go?"

"He'll turn up all right."

"Is dying hard, Daddy?"

"No, I think it's pretty easy, Nick. It all depends."

They were seated in the boat, Nick in the stern, his father rowing. The sun was coming up over the hills. A bass jumped, making a circle in the water. Nick trailed his hand in the water. It felt warm in the sharp chill of the morning.

In the early morning on the lake sitting in the stern of the boat with his father rowing, he felt quite sure that he would never die.

I'D DARE TO MAKE more mistakes next time. I'd relax, I would limber up. I would be sillier than I have been this trip. I would take fewer things seriously. I would take more chances. I would climb more mountains and swim more rivers. I would eat more ice cream and less beans. I would perhaps have more actual troubles, but I'd have fewer imaginary ones.

You see, I'm one of those people who live sensibly and sanely hour after hour, day after day. Oh, I've had my

If I Had My Life to Live Over
BY NADINE STAIR

moments, and if I had it to do over again, I'd have more of them. In fact, I'd try to have nothing else. Just moments, one after another, instead of living so many years ahead of each day. I've been one of those persons who never goes anywhere without a thermometer, a hot water bottle, a raincoat and a parachute. If I had to do it again, I would travel lighter than I have.

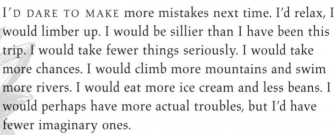

If I had my life live over, I would start barefoot earlier in the spring and stay that way later in the fall. I would go to more dances. I would ride more merry-go-rounds. I would pick more daisies.

What A Wonderful World

WORDS AND MUSIC BY GEORGE DAVID WEISS AND BOB THIELE

I see trees of green, red roses too,
I see them bloom for me and you,
And I think to myself
What a wonderful world.

I see skies of blue and clouds of white,
The bright blessed day, the dark sacred night,
And I think to myself
What a wonderful world.

The colors of the rainbow, so pretty in the sky
Are also on the faces of people goin' by,
I see friends shakin' hands, sayin', "How do you do!"
They're really sayin' "I love you,"
I hear babies cry, I watch them grow
They'll learn much more than I'll ever know
And I think to myself
What a wonderful world.

Yes, I think to myself
What a wonderful world.

ANN RICHARDS

MOUNT HOLYOKE COLLEGE
MAY 28, 1995

...WHEN THE STRUGGLE SEEMS LONG and difficult, it might be useful to remember what Thurgood Marshall told us: that it is not only how far we have come but how close we are. Your role in shaping public policy is vital to our future. Now as you set off on that drive, I thought the least I could do is to offer a little personal advice to you. Now that the preaching is over, I thought I should give you five rules for living that have worked for me.

The first rule in life is: Cherish your friends and family as if your life depended on it. Because it does.

Number two: Love people more than things. You know those T-shirts that say "He who dies with the most toys wins." I'm going to promise you that over the years I've spent my life collecting a great number of things I thought I would die without. And I wouldn't give you a nickel for most of it today.

Number three: Indulge the fool in you. Encourage the clown and the laughter that is inside of you. Go ahead and do it! Make time for play, for the impractical, for the absurd, and make it a rule to do it. Not just every now and then. Let your heart overrule your head once in a while. Never turn down a new experience unless it's against the law or will get you in serious trouble.

Number four: Don't spend a lot of time worrying about your failures. I've learned a whole lot more from my mistakes than from all my successes.

And number five: Have some sense about work. No one ever died muttering, "I wish I spent more time at the office."

There is a wonderful world out there. It's just waiting for your energy and your ideas. We need you.

God bless you and Godspeed.

If you can't do it with love and cheerfulness, don't do it at all—go home.

MOTHER TERESA

i thank You God for most this amazing

E.E. CUMMINGS

i thank You God for most this amazing
day:for the leaping greenly spirits of trees
and a blue true dream of sky;and for everything
which is natural which is infinite which is yes

(i who have died am alive again today,
and this is the sun's birthday;this is the birth
day of life and of love and wings:and of the gay
great happening illimitably earth)

how should tasting touching hearing seeing
breathing any—lifted from the no
of all nothing—human merely being
doubt unimaginable You?

(now the ears of my ears awake and
now the eyes of my eyes are opened)

DEAR DIARY

"Above all, you must illuminate your own soul, with all its profundities and its shallows, and its vanities and its generosities, and say what your beauty means to you, or your plainness, and what your relation is to the ever-changing and turning world of gloves and shoes and stuff swaying up and down."
–Virginia Woolf (1882–1941), *A Room of One's Own*

Why do people keep diaries? Is writing about yourself a narcissistic enterprise by definition? Can writing about your most intimate thoughts, daily happenings, and special events have any redeeming value? How do you decide what to write about?

Diaries and journals are not merely books in which to write your daily activities. For most people, this practice would lead to a very bland record, unworthy of being read, even by its owner. Rather, diary writing, when treated as a discipline, is a record of your development and growth—a personal report card.

Whether you are using your diary for self-discovery, to develop creativity, to escape from the craziness of life, to chronicle your life for a future autobiography, to solve problems, to become more organized, to gain emotional perspective, or as a form of therapy, using these tips can enrich your diary writing so you can better track your progress.

TIPS ON KEEPING A DIARY:

Try to find at least five minutes a day to write.

Keep a pocket diary (a small notepad) with you to jot down thoughts or observations that you can later transfer into your diary.

Date your pages.

When time permits, write a short paragraph about current events to set your entry in a larger context.

The more honest you are with yourself in your diary, the more closely your entries will reflect who you are.

Mix up the form of your writing now and then (e.g., write a story about yourself or record your stream of consciousness).

After you have finished an entry, either create a title for it, or write a "thought of the day" at the top of your page.

Don't reread your entries until at least a month has passed. This should give you enough time to gain perspective on your writing.

ANNE FRANK TO HER DIARY, KITTY

MARCH 7, 1944

Dear Kitty,

If I think now of my life in 1942, it all seems so unreal. It was quite a different Anne who enjoyed that heavenly existence from the Anne who has grown wise within these walls. Yes, it was a heavenly life. Boy friends at every turn, about twenty friends and acquaintances of my own age, the darling of nearly all the teachers, spoiled from top to toe by Mummy and Daddy, lots of sweets, enough pocket money, what more could one want?

   You will certainly wonder by what means I got around all these people. Peter's word "attractiveness" is not altogether true. All the teachers were entertained by my cute answers, my amusing remarks, my smiling face, and my questioning looks.

That is all I was—a terrible flirt, coquettish and amusing. I had one or two advantages, which kept me rather in favor. I was industrious, honest, and frank. I would never have dreamed of cribbing from anyone else. I shared my sweets generously, and I wasn't conceited.

Wouldn't I have become rather forward with so much admiration? It was a good thing that in the midst of, at the height of, all this gaiety, I suddenly had to face reality, and it took me at least a year to get used to the fact that there was no more admiration forthcoming.

How did I appear at school? The one who thought of new jokes and pranks, always "king of the castle," never in a bad mood, never a crybaby. No wonder everyone liked to cycle with me, and I got their attentions.

Now I look back at that Anne as an amusing, but very superficial girl, who has nothing to do with the Anne of today. Peter said quite rightly about me: "If ever I saw you, you were always surrounded by two or more boys and a whole troupe of girls. You were always laughing and always the center of everything!"

What is left of this girl? Oh, don't worry, I haven't forgotten how to laugh or to answer back readily. I'm just as good, if not better, at criticizing people, and I can still flirt if…I wish. That's not it though, I'd like that sort of life again for an evening, a few days, or even a week; the life which seems so carefree and gay. But at the end of that week, I should be dead beat and would be only too thankful to listen to anyone who began to talk about something sensible. I don't want followers, but friends, admirers who fall not for a flattering smile but for what one does and for one's character.

I know quite well that the circle around me would be much smaller. But what does that matter, as long as one still keeps a few sincere friends?

Yet I wasn't entirely happy in 1942 in spite of everything; I often felt deserted, but because I was on the go the whole day long, I didn't think about it and enjoyed myself as much as I could. Consciously or unconsciously, I tried to drive away the emptiness I felt with jokes and pranks. Now I think seriously about life and what I have to do. One period of my life is over forever. The carefree schooldays are gone, never to return.

I don't even long for them any more; I have outgrown them,
I can't just only enjoy myself as my serious side is always there.

I look upon my life up till the New Year, as it were, through a
powerful magnifying glass. The sunny life at home, then coming
here in 1942, the sudden change, the quarrels, the bickerings.
I couldn't understand it, I was taken by surprise, and the only
way I could keep up some bearing was by being impertinent.

The first half of 1943: my fits of crying, the loneliness, how I
slowly began to see all my faults and shortcomings, which are so
great and which seemed much greater then. During the day I
deliberately talked about anything and everything that was
farthest from my thoughts, tried to draw Pim to me; but
couldn't. Alone I had to face the difficult task of changing myself,
to stop the everlasting reproaches, which were so oppressive and
which reduced me to such terrible despondency.

Things improved slightly in the second half of the year,
I became a young woman and was treated more like a grownup.
I started to think, and write stories, and came to the conclusion
that the others no longer had the right to throw me about like

an india-rubber ball. I wanted to change in accordance with my own desires. But ONE thing that struck me even more was when I realized that even Daddy would never become my confidant over everything. I didn't want to trust anyone but myself any more.

At the beginning of the New Year: the second great change, my dream....And with it I discovered my longing, not for a girl friend, but for a boy friend. I also discovered my inward happiness and my defensive armor of superficiality and gaiety. In due time I quieted down and discovered my boundless desire for all that is beautiful and good.

And in the evening, when I lie in bed and end my prayers with the words, "I thank you, God, for all that is good and dear and beautiful," I am filled with joy. Then I think about "the good" of going into hiding, of my health and with my whole being of the "dearness" of Peter, of that which is still embryonic and impressionable and which we neither of us dare to name or touch, of that which will come sometime; love, the future, happiness and of "the beauty" which exists in the world; the world, nature, beauty and all, all that is exquisite and fine.

I don't think then of all the misery, but of the beauty that still remains. This is one of the things that Mummy and I are so entirely different about. Her counsel when one feels melancholy is: "Think of all the misery in the world and be thankful that you are not sharing in it!" My advice is: "Go outside, to the fields, enjoy nature and the sunshine, go out and try to recapture happiness in yourself and in God. Think of all the beauty that's still left in and around you and be happy!"

I don't see how Mummy's idea can be right, because then how are you supposed to behave if you go through the misery yourself? Then you are lost. On the contrary, I've found that there is always some beauty left—in nature, sunshine, freedom, in yourself; these can all help you. Look at these things, then you find yourself again, and God, and then you regain your balance.

And whoever is happy will make others happy too. He who has courage and faith will never perish in misery!

Yours, Anne

from ALL I REALLY NEED TO KNOW I LEARNED IN KINDERGARTEN

By Robert Fulghum

GIANTS, WIZARDS, AND DWARFS was the game to play.

Being left in charge of about eighty children seven to ten years old, while their parents were off doing parenty things, I mustered my troops in the church social hall and explained the game. It's a large-scale version of Rock, Paper, and Scissors, and involves some intellectual decision making. But the real purpose of the game is to make a lot of noise and run around chasing people until nobody knows which side you are on or who won.

Organizing a roomful of wired-up gradeschoolers into two teams, explaining the rudiments of the game, achieving consensus on group identity—all this is no mean accomplishment, but we did it with a right good will and were ready to go.

The excitement of the chase had reached a critical mass. I yelled out: "You have to decide *now* which you are—a GIANT, a WIZARD, or a DWARF!"

While the groups huddled in frenzied, whispered consultation, a tug came at my pants leg. A small child stands there looking up,

and asks in a small, concerned voice, "Where do the Mermaids stand?"

Where do the Mermaids stand?

A long pause. A *very* long pause. "Where do the Mermaids stand?" says I.

"Yes. You see, I am a Mermaid."

"There are no such things as Mermaids."

"Oh, yes, I am one!"

She did not relate to being a Giant, a Wizard, or a Dwarf. She knew her category. Mermaid. And was not about to leave the game and go over and stand against the wall where a loser would stand. She intended to participate, wherever Mermaids fit into the scheme of things. Without giving up dignity or identity. She took it for granted that there was a place for Mermaids and that I would know just where.

Well, where DO the Mermaids stand? All the "Mermaids"—all those who are different, who do not fit the norm and who do not accept the available boxes and pigeonholes?

Answer that question and you can build a school, a nation, or a world on it.

What was my answer at the moment? Every once in a while I say the right thing. "The Mermaid stands right here by the King

of the Sea!" says I. (*Yes, right here by the King's Fool, I thought to myself.*)

So we stood there hand in hand, reviewing the troops of Wizards and Giants and Dwarfs as they roiled by in wild disarray.

It is not true, by the way, that mermaids do not exist. I know at least one personally. I have held her hand.

There ain't no answer.
There ain't going to be any answer.
There never has been an answer.
That's the answer.

GERTRUDE STEIN

I CAN DO ANYTHING. I can be anything. No one ever told me I couldn't. No one ever expressed this idea that I was limited to any one thing, and so I think in terms of what's possible, not impossible.

Dream

BY WHOOPI GOLDBERG

They did sell me on the notion of reality. That I got. I got the laws of physics and nature pretty much down and knew early on there were very specific things I couldn't do. I knew I could never make anyone float, or turn water into wine, or make cats speak French. I knew I couldn't bring people back from the dead. I got that part of it. But I also knew that if I was with someone who had lost somebody I might be able to make them feel better. I couldn't keep someone's house from burning down, but I could help them sort through the rubble and get their shit together and start in on another one. So I realized I wasn't God, which was a slight disappointment, you know. Just a slight disappointment—and a mild surprise.

Movies were my first window to the outside world, and they told me stuff. They told me I could go anywhere,

be whatever I wanted, solve any damn puzzle. The right movie was my ticket to any place I wanted to go. But it had to be the right movie, and it had to come from the right place, 'cause I had to bank on it being historically accurate. See, in school, nobody talked about black people unless they had us picking cotton. Who knew there were free blacks? Maybe you heard about Frederick Douglass, but you didn't really know about Frederick Douglass. You couldn't always trust the history books. They told a diluted truth, a truth by committee. It was only later that I learned there was something missing in what went down with the landed Americans and the indigenous people of this country. In movies too. They didn't always get the story right, especially when it came to our nonwhite history. You knew the Indians didn't look like Jeffrey Hunter, but you didn't know what they really looked like either. It was a great mystery. There weren't too many Indians in my Catholic school in New York, so you had to use your imagination a little bit.

In my head, Queen Elizabeth was just like Bette Davis. That's how I saw her. She walked and talked and *poofed*— and made grand statements in staccato sentences. Movies opened doors to a lot of things for me, but for every one they opened another one closed. The casting always messed with the way I saw it. It changed the terms. In this way, books were more liberating, more magical, and so I started to read. To really *read*. Books opened the mind to all kinds of possibilities. There is nothing in Dickens to leave you thinking there were no black people in England, or that Bob Cratchit didn't pass you on the street every single day. But movies made you believe there were no black people, except the ones who were picking cotton, or tap-dancing up a flight of stairs, or birthin' babies. When I was little, this didn't strike me as odd, but as I grew up, all during the 1960s, it bothered the *#@*! out of me. I knew there had to be more to us than that. Now I know there are all-black movies, with gumshoes and heroes, cowboys and harlots, but these were just not shown on the *Million Dollar Movie*, and when I started to figure this out I realized life was what we put in and took out, and we were all in the same soup. Indians, blacks, Asians, women…It never even occurred to me that Emma *wasn't* black. It wasn't a part of the equation. Why shouldn't we have been in a Jane Austen situation?

Why wouldn't we have been in a manor house in a Dickens novel? Why couldn't we have been the light in the forest? And don't tell me Robert Louis Stevenson didn't have me in mind when he wrote *Treasure Island*, because, you know, even the Muppets understand this notion.

Daydreaming, I used to think I was Sherlock Holmes; it's a part I've always wanted to play. If you're the most brilliant detective, the people will come to you. They won't care if you're black, or a woman. It might even give the story some new dimensions. *The Speckled Band*, starring Whoopi Goldberg. I like it!

This—the possibility—is why I look on acting as such a joyous thing. It's shot through with possibility. Anything can happen. As I write this, I'm appearing eight times a week, on Broadway, in a part originally written for a man, but you'd never know, right? If you come to a thing with no preconceived notions of what that thing is, the whole world can be your canvas. Just dream it, and you can make it so. I believe I belong wherever I want to be, in whatever situation or context I place myself. I believed I could pass as an ancient Roman in *A Funny Thing Happened on the Way to the Forum*. I believed a little girl could rise from a single-parent household in the Manhattan projects, start a single-parent household of her own, struggle through seven years of welfare and odd jobs, and still wind up making movies. You can go from anonymity to Planet Hollywood and never lose sight of where you've been.

So, yeah, I think anything is possible. I know it because I have lived it. I know it because I have seen it. I have witnessed things the ancients would have called miracles, but they are not miracles. They are the products of someone's dream, and they happen as the result of hard work. Or they happen because, you know, [stuff] happens. As human beings, we are capable of creating a paradise, and making each other's lives better by our own hands. Yes, yes, yes…this is possible.

If something hasn't happened, it's not because it can't happen, or won't; it just hasn't happened yet. If I haven't done something, I just haven't gotten around to it. For a long time, I wanted to sit with Stephen Hawking and have him explain all his theories to me so that I could understand them and build on them and find ways to adapt them to my own life. But I never got around to that. I would like to be a diplomat in some foreign country for a couple months. I would like to play for the Knicks, and dance with Alvin Ailey, and ride a camel down Sunset Boulevard. I would like to find a way to stop famine, and to free the children from the orphanages in Bosnia, Rwanda, and Romania, and here at home. I would like to do a lot of things. All I need is time.

Changes

WORDS AND MUSIC BY DAVID BOWIE

I still don't know what I was waiting for
and my time was running wild.
A million dead-end streets,
and every time I thought I'd got it made,
it seemed the taste was not so sweet.

So I turned myself to face me
But I've never caught a glimpse of how the
    others must see the faker
I'm much too fast to take that test.
(Ch—ch—ch—ch—chan—ges)
Turn and face the stranger
(Ch—ch—chan—ges)
Don't want to be a richer man.
(Ch—ch—ch—ch—chan—ges)
Turn and face the stranger
(Ch-ch-chan - ges)
Just gonna have to be a different man.
Time may change me, but I can't trace time.

(Interlude)
Strange fascination, fascinating me
Changes are taking the pace I'm going thru
(Ch—ch—ch—ch—chan—ges)
    Turn and face the stranger
(Ch—ch—chan—ges)
Oh look out you rock 'n' rollers
(Ch—ch—ch—ch—chan—ges)
    turn and face the stranger
(Ch—ch—chan—ges)
Pretty soon now you're gonna get older
Time may change me
    But I can't trace time
I said that time may change me,
    but I can't trace time

I watch the ripples change their size,
    but never leave the stream
Of warm impermanence and so the days
    flow thru my eyes
But still the days seem the same.
And these children that you spit on
    as they try to change their worlds
Are immune to your consultations, they're
    quite aware of what they're going thru'

(Ch—ch—ch—ch—Changes)
    Turn and face the stranger
(Ch—ch—changes)
    Don't tell them to grow up and out of it,
(Ch—ch—ch—ch—Changes)
    Turn and face the stranger
(Ch—ch—changes)
    where's your shame, you've left us up to
    our necks in it
Time may change me,
    but you can't trace time. (To Interlude)

JODIE FOSTER

YALE UNIVERSITY
MAY 23, 1993

...THE TWENTIES FOR ME were about learning to trust my instincts above all else. Being inside the dance without continual awareness of the choreography. That's the most essential quality you can have as an actor and a director. The ability to dive headfirst into an unknown body of water and commit to the current with a lot of faith, no hesitation, and a big, fat smile on your face.

Now somewhere along the way I started looking over my shoulder and noticing a pattern and my work starting to take a shape. It wasn't just about being hungry for more, it wasn't about being richer or having whiter teeth than the guy before. It was about completing a recognizable spiritual and psychological agenda. So yes, I recognized the method to my madness. For example, I was compelled to play characters who had been overlooked, misunderstood, marginalized, victimized, or labeled as freaks. But they survive in the end. I wanted people to recognize the humanity of these characters and decide for themselves, to redeem them, and in turn simply get better because of that self-acknowledgment and self-acceptance. Now that's perhaps very foolish and naive—so what? That's why they call it the movies.

My Yale experience has given me the luxury of choice. I've chosen to make my life, my work, my love, my characters stand for something, however small and insignificant that legacy may be. And each one of you will have your own way, your own

battles, your own processes. But ultimately it's up to you alone to find the way that's appropriate for you. No one can tell you what that is because no one else has ever been there before. You find your way home again. My way has brought me toward a narrowing focus at the beginning of my thirties. I want to change the system from within the system. And that means focusing and specializing. I can't fight every monster, every ogre anymore. I've got to be precise. So you know I don't read three newspapers a day. I don't know a lot about music anymore or important current events that are shaping our nation. I don't know very much about some very basic things. But if you start talking about weird French films from the seventies or the latest studio merger, I'm liable to go off and get all sweaty and indignant and passionate. Telling stories—that's my Olympic event. That's the revolution I choose to fight in. And you're no good to the revolution if you're dead or unprepared.

So what exactly did I want to pass on to you? What personal agenda do I bring to this sort of throwing of the caps and smoking of the pipe and donning of the gown? I want you to continue living. Continue searching harder, deeper, faster, stronger, and louder and knowing that one day you'll be called upon to use all that you've amassed in the process. With that wealth of self-knowledge, you hold all of our futures in your hands. So you better make it good. You better keep your eyes open and your hearts open and find out what's beneath the surface. What moves you, what repels you, and what compels you. Become human first and identify what exactly that is later. Let how you live your life stand for something, no matter how small and incidental it may seem. Because it's not good enough to put change in the meter without questioning what the meter's doing there in

the first place. It's not good enough to let life pass you by in the name of some greater glory. This is it. This is all you get. So love this life, curse this life and claim this life for your very own. Do it for yourself, do it for the Fat Lady hiding in the ivy, smiling and waving and laughing at the absurdity of all this. She'll be dancing with you tonight, jiggling her body this way and that to some funky hip-hop graduation haze. She'll go on following you year after year, sitting in the back rows, beaming proudly, loving you unconditionally, and all that she asks is that you choose the becoming. And you do that alone, but in her gaze.

Now you have fun. Breathe deeply and kick ass in the process.

From **HAMLET**

By William Shakespeare

To be, or not to be, that is the question:
Whether 'tis nobler in the mind to suffer
The slings and arrows of outrageous fortune,
Or to take arms against a sea of troubles
And by opposing end them. To die—to sleep,
No more; and by a sleep to say we end
The heart-ache and the thousand natural shocks
That flesh is heir to: 'tis a consummation
Devoutly to be wish'd. To die, to sleep;
To sleep, perchance to dream—ay, there's the rub:
For in that sleep of death what dreams may come,
When we have shuffled off this mortal coil,
Must give us pause—there's the respect
That makes calamity of so long life.
For who would bear the whips and scorns of time,
Th'oppressor's wrong, the proud man's contumely,
The pangs of dispriz'd love, the law's delay,
The insolence of office, and the spurns

HAMLET

That patient merit of th'unworthy takes,
When he himself might his quietus make
With a bare bodkin? Who would fardels bear,
To grunt and sweat under a weary life,
But that the dread of something after death,
The undiscover'd country, from whose bourn
No traveller returns, puzzles the will,
And makes us rather bear those ills we have
Than fly to others that we know not of?
Thus conscience does make cowards of us all,
And thus the native hue of resolution
Is sicklied o'er with the pale cast of thought,
And enterprises of great pitch and moment
With this regard their currents turn awry
And lose the name of action.

Résumé

BY DOROTHY PARKER

Razors pain you;

Rivers are damp;

Acids stain you;

And drugs cause cramp.

Guns aren't lawful;

Nooses give;

Gas smells awful;

You might as well live.

One can never consent
to creep when one feels
an impulse to soar.

HELEN KELLER

To see a World
in a Grain of Sand

BY WILLIAM BLAKE

To see a World in a Grain of Sand

And a Heaven in a Wild Flower,

Hold Infinity in the palm of your hand

And Eternity in an hour.

AWAKEN YOUR SPIRIT

What is spirituality? Do you have to be religious to enjoy a spiritual life? Are prayers reserved for the devout? Do you have to have a specific need in order to pray? How do you cultivate spirituality in your personal life?

Spirituality has many forms and fills many needs. Some people find great joy and comfort in the structure and support of organized religion. They find that belonging to a community with others who share their religious and spiritual beliefs offers a sense of purpose and the tools to cope with the challenges of life. Others prefer to explore their spiritual life in more solitary, meditative surroundings. They contemplate their values and the questions of existence in their own ways. There is no right way to go about kindling your own spirit. Whatever your goals for your personal spirituality, make time for nurturing that aspect of your life. Here are some ways to tap into your spirit:

Define your essential values and test how closely you stick to them. Ask yourself: What is most important to me? Do I make time for the things that matter most? Am I distracted by lesser "obligations" and so neglect what truly matters? How closely do my daily activities represent my values?

Read inspirational literature and listen to spiritual music—according to your own tastes, of course. You might gravitate toward Rainer Maria Rilke's poetry, while your best friend is uplifted by the words of Dr. Martin Luther King. Your neighbor may love the sound of Gregorian chanting, while you prefer listening to Beethoven's Fifth Symphony.

Let the world around you comfort and inspire you. Admire nature's beauty. Walk on the beach or hike in the mountains. Gaze into the star-filled sky.

Strive to see the extraordinary in ordinary things—the wonder in a child's eyes, the smile on the face of a stranger, or the delicate blossoms on a cherry tree.

Make time each day for prayer or meditation. Relaxation techniques can help keep you grounded and centered on your values.

> *I cannot teach you how to pray in words…and I cannot teach*
> *you the prayer of the seas and the forests and the mountains.*
> *But you who are born of the mountains and the forests and*
> *the seas can find their prayer in your heart.*
>
> —Kahlil Gibran, The Prophet

Prayer and meditation contain the dual powers of healing and imparting energy. You can pray in times of distress, but also as thanks for life's joys. Pray for family, friends, and for the Earth. Use a talisman if you find it helps you focus your thoughts. Here are some prayers from around the world:

With your feet I walk
I walk with your limbs
I carry forth your body
For me your mind thinks
Your voice speaks for me
Beauty is before me
And beauty is behind me
Above and below me hovers the beautiful
I am surrounded by it
I am immersed in it
In my youth I am aware of it
And in old age I shall walk quietly
The beautiful trail.

–Navajo Prayer

Do not seek too much fame,
but do not seek obscurity.
Be proud.
But do not remind the world of your deeds.
Excel when you must,
but do not excel the world.
Many heroes are not yet born,
many have already died.
To be alive to hear this song is a victory.

–West African Song

Deep peace of the running wave to you.
Deep peace of the flowing air to you.
Deep peace of the quiet earth to you.
Deep peace of the shining stars to you.
Deep peace of the infinite peace to you.

–Gaelic Blessing

Blessed are the poor in spirit:
for theirs is the kingdom of heaven.
Blessed are they that mourn:
for they shall be comforted.
Blessed are the meek:
for they shall inherit the earth.
Blessed are they which do hunger and
thirst after righteousness:
for they shall be filled.
Blessed are the merciful:
for they shall obtain mercy.
Blessed are the pure in heart:
for they shall see God.
Blessed are the peacemakers:
for they shall be called the children of God.
Blessed are they which are persecuted for
righteousness' sake:
for theirs is the kingdom of heaven.

–Matthew 5:3-10

When you were born, you cried
and the world rejoiced.
Live your life in such a way
that when you die, the world cries
and you rejoice.

INDIAN SAYING

A Child of Mine

BY SCOTT EYERLY

I can see

Reflections in your eyes

One of me

And one of distant skies.

You are leaving

But part of me goes with you

Near or far, you are a child of mine.

Author Anne Morrow Lindbergh to her husband, Charles

July 2, 1944

Dear Charles,

I am on my way West. I hope to meet you. I feel madly extravagant and altogether quite mad, speeding over the country with not much certainty of when or where I'll meet you.

But I feel happy tonight. I have sat and watched the cornfields of Iowa darken, seen the homesteads pass by—a white house, a red barn and a brave cluster of green trees in the midst of oceans of flat fields—like an oasis in a desert. The glossy flanks of horses and the glossy leaves of corn. And I have been overcome by the beauty and richness of this country I have flown over so many times with you. And overcome with the beauty and richness of our life together, those early mornings setting out, those evenings gleaming with rivers and lakes below us, still holding the last light. Those fields of daisies we landed on—and dusty fields and desert stretches. Memories of many skies and many earths beneath us—many days, many nights of stars. "How are the waters of the world sweet—if we should die, we have drunk them. If we should sin—or separate— if we should fail or secede—we have tasted of happiness—we must be written in the book of the blessed. We have had what life could give, we have eaten of the tree of knowledge, we have known—we have been the mystery of the universe."

Good night—

Ulysses

BY ALFRED LORD TENNYSON

It little profits that an idle king,
By this still hearth, among these barren crags,
Matched with an aged wife, I mete and dole
Unequal laws unto a savage race,
The hoard, and sleep, and feed, and know not me.
I cannot rest from travel; I will drink
Life to the lees. All times I have enjoyed
Greatly, have suffered greatly, both with those
That loved me, and alone; on shore, and when
Through scudding drifts the rainy Hyades
Vext the dim sea. I am become a name;
For always roaming with a hungry heart
Much have I seen and known,—cities of men
And manners, climates, councils, governments,
Myself not least, but honoured of them all,—
And drunk delight of battle with my peers,
Far on the ringing plains of windy Troy.
I am part of all that I have met;
Yet all experiences is an arch wherethrough
Gleams that untravelled world whose margin fades
For ever and for ever when I move.

How dull it is to pause, to make an end,
To rust unburnished, not to shine in use!
As though to breathe were life! Life piled on life
Were all to little, and of one to me
Little remains; but every hour is saved
From that eternal silence, something more,
A bringer of new things; and vile it were
For some three sums to store and hoard myself,
And this gray spirit yearning in desire
To follow knowledge like a sinking star,
Beyond the utmost bound of human thought.

This is my son, mine own Telemachus,
To whom I leave the sceptre and the isle,—
Well-loved of me, discerning to fulfill
This labour, by slow prudence to make mild
A rugged people, and through soft degrees
Subdue them to the useful and the good.
Most blameless is he, centred in the sphere
Of common duties, decent not to fail
In offices of tenderness, and pay
Meet adoration to my household gods,
When I am gone. He works his work, I mine.
There lies the port; the vessel puffs her sail;
There gloom the dark, broad seas. My mariners,

Souls that have toiled and wrought, and thought with me,—
That ever with a frolic welcome took
The thunder and the sunshine, and opposed
Free hearts, free foreheads,—you and I are old;
Old age hath yet his honour and his toil.
Death closes all; but something ere the end,
Some work of noble note, may yet be done,
Not unbecoming men that strove with Gods.
The lights begin to twinkle from the rocks;
The long day wanes; the slow moon climbs; the deep
Moans round with many voices. Come, my friends,
'Tis not too late to seek a newer world.
Push off, and sitting well in order smite
The sounding furrows; for my purpose holds
To sail beyond the sunset, and the baths
Of all the western stars, until I die.
It may be that the gulfs will wash us down;
It may be we shall tough the Happy Isles,
And see the great Achilles, whom we knew.
Though much is taken, much abides; and though
We are not now that strength which in old days
Moved earth and heaven, that which we are, we are,—
One equal temper of heroic hearts,
Made weak by time and fate, but strong in will
To survive, to seek, to find, and not to yield.

from PETER PAN

BY J. M. BARRIE

ALL CHILDREN, EXCEPT ONE, GROW UP. They soon know that they will grow up, and the way Wendy knew was this. One day when she was two years old she was playing in a garden, and she plucked another flower and ran with it to her mother. I suppose she must have looked rather delightful, for Mrs. Darling put her hand to her heart and cried, "Oh, why can't you remain like this for ever!" This was all that passed between them on the subject, but henceforth Wendy knew that she must grow up. You always know after you are two. Two is the beginning of the end.

Be sober and vigilant.
Remember at all times that
while you are seeing the world,
the world will see you.

BENJAMIN & JULIA RUSH
(IN A LETTER TO THEIR SON, JOHN)

DURING OUR COLLEGE YEARS, I asked the man who is now my husband for the same gift for Valentine's Day, my birthday, and Christmas. He would say, "What do you want?" And I would reply, "An engagement ring." And he would laugh. In no time at all this became a standing joke, which is why, on my twenty-fifth birthday, I opened the latest in a succession of tiny boxes that had previously contained earrings, lockets, and the like with an air that was just a little bit lackadaisical. Inside the box was an engagement ring. Life had sneaked up behind me and planted a kiss on my cheek just as I had finally stopped straining to hear its footfalls. I wasn't looking for it, and so it came.

Tuning Forks

BY ANNA QUINDLEN

I know there are people who never strain, who go to look at houses they want to buy armed with a notebook, a list of practical questions, and a dignified, slightly critical manner. I know there are people who can argue about salary at job interviews and those who can greet a blind date—even one described by friends as a tall neurosurgeon with a great sense of humor—with a firm handshake and a level look.

And then there are people like me. I like to think of us as the tuning forks. When we are in the market for anything of substance—an apartment, a job, a relationship, a dress to wear on New Year's Eve—we give off a high-pitched tone akin to that emitted by dog whistles. This tone sends one of two messages to people: stay away, or take us for all we are worth. Most women have known a fair number of allegedly eligible men in each category (and some who started out in the second and then moved rapidly to the first). But of the rental agents and personnel managers I've known, most were the take-'em type. The only exception was the wonderful, cynical man who once interviewed me for a reporter's job and who, when I said I would work for free, answered coldly, "Don't be dramatic."

The tuning-fork phenomenon gives life an interesting quality, which, according to some friends, was introduced early in their own lives by their mothers. If you want something, it will elude you. If you do not want something, you will get ten of it in the mail. I have become such a firm believer in this that now that I have a place to live I half expect doormen all over New York City to dart forward as I pass by, grab my arm and say, "The penthouse just opened up—it has four bedrooms and a terrace, and the fireplace works."

This is in sharp contrast to the search for my first apartment, which took place with my pupils permanently dilated with desperation and desire, one of the telltale signs of tuning forks everywhere. I told agents that I didn't care if

the bathtub was in the kitchen, didn't mind if there wasn't a kitchen at all, and thought the walk-in closet would indeed, with a little work, make a lovely bedroom. When I finally found a human habitation for rent, nothing could dissuade me. The delay on delivery of the refrigerator? (I'm getting a refrigerator? God! How great!) The hole in the bedroom ceiling? (I'll only see it when I'm lying down.) The rent? (It's reasonable. Or it would be if I had it. But I'll get it.)

Of course I adored that apartment because I had wanted it so badly, wanted it for no reason except that I was looking and it was there, which as many women can tell you is a key to some inexplicable and horrible relationships. During a time when I was in flux on just about every level, that apartment was my safe haven. I remember how, starting off from that apartment, I would take long walks around the city streets, in jeans and sneakers, buying flowers and food, window shopping, watching the pickup basketball games and the kids in the park. I thought this was all quite casual and continental, and that if I did it long enough I would meet some people. One morning a coworker said he had seen me walking the evening before and that he almost hadn't recognized me. "You looked so intense," he said. "You sort of looked like a cross between one of those kids with the big eyes in Keane paintings, and a serial murderer." No wonder I wasn't meeting anyone.

I was thinking about this the other night because of what happened on the bus. A man sat down next to me. I was reading my newspaper and he was reading his, and after a few minutes he started an idle conversation about some news event. That's when I noticed how handsome he was. In the course of the conversation, it also occurred to me that he was quite smart. When he asked if I had had dinner, I realized he was trying to pick me up.

Under other circumstances—say, if I had not had a husband and two small children at home waiting for me— this would have been marvelous, but under other circumstances this would not have happened. It crossed my mind that it was a function of age, that I was only so crazed when I was younger because I was younger, but I don't believe it's so. If I were still looking, that man would have changed seats or feigned sleep or keeled over in a fake faint rather than talk to me. He would have heard the hum. He would have known that he could tell me he'd like to have dinner, but wanted to warn me that he was leaving the next day to join the Green Berets for a secret training mission in Lebanon, and that in response I would have said only two words: "Which restaurant?"

Over the Rainbow

BY HAROLD ARLEN AND E.Y. HARBURG

When all the world is a hopeless jumble and
    the raindrops tumble all around,
Heaven opens a magic lane.
When all the clouds darken up the skyway,
    there's a rainbow highway to be found,
Leading from your window pane.
To a place behind the sun,
Just a step beyond the rain.

Somewhere over the rainbow way up high,
There's a land that I heard of once in a lullaby,
Somewhere over the rainbow skies are blue,
And the dreams that you dare to dream really do come true.

Someday I'll wish upon a star and wake up
    where the clouds are far behind me,
Where troubles melt like lemon drops, away above the chimney tops
    that's where you'll find me.
Somewhere over the rainbow bluebirds fly,
Birds fly over the rainbow, why then, oh why can't I?

If happy little bluebirds fly beyond the rainbow, why, oh why, can't I?

BARBARA BUSH

WELLESLEY COLLEGE
JUNE 1, 1990

IN THE WORLD THAT AWAITS YOU beyond the shores of Lake Waban, no one can say what your true colors will be. But this I do know. You have a first-class education from a first-class school. And so you need not, probably cannot, live a paint-by-numbers life. Decisions are not irrevocable. Choices do come back. And as you set off from Wellesley, I hope that many of you will consider making three very specific choices.

The first is to believe in something larger than yourself. Get involved in some of the big ideas of our time. I chose literacy because I honestly believe that if more people could read, write, and comprehend, we would be that much closer to solving so many of the problems that plague our nation and our society.

Early on I made another choice, which I hope you will make as well. Whether you are talking about education, career or service, you are talking about life. And life must really have joy. It's supposed to be fun.

One of the reasons I made the most important decision of my life...to marry George Bush...is because he made me laugh. It's true, sometimes we've laughed through our tears. But that shared laughter has been one of our strongest bonds. Find the joy in life, because as Ferris Bueller said on his day off, "Life moves pretty fast, ya don't stop to look around once in awhile, ya gonna miss it!" I am not going to tell George you clapped more for Ferris than you did for George!

The third choice that must not be missed is to cherish your human connections, your relationships with family and friends. For several years, you've had impressed upon you the importance of your career of dedication and hard work, and of course that's true. But as important as your obligations as a doctor, lawyer, or business leader will be, you are a human being first, and those human connections with spouses, with children, with friends are the most important investments you will ever make.

At the end of your life you will never regret not having passed one more test, not winning one more verdict, or not closing one more deal. You will regret time not spent with a husband, a child, a friend, or a parent.

We are in a transitional period right now, a fascinating and exhilarating time, learning to adjust to the changes and the choices we men and women are facing. As an example I remember what a friend said on hearing her husband complain to his buddies that he had to baby-sit. Quickly setting him straight, my friend told her husband that when it's your own kids, it's not called baby-sitting!

Maybe we should adjust faster; maybe we should adjust slower. But whatever the era, whatever the times, one thing will never change: Fathers and mothers, if you have children, they must come first. You must read to your children. Your success as a family, our success as a society depends not on what happens in the White House but on what happens inside your house.

...Thank you. God bless you, and may your future be worthy of your dreams.

When I was a young man, I wanted to change the world. I found it was difficult to change the world, so I tried to change my nation. When I found I couldn't change the nation, I began to focus on my town. I couldn't change the town, and as an older man, I tried to change my family. Now, as an old man, I realize the only thing I can change is myself, and suddenly I realize that if long ago I had changed myself, I could have made an impact on my family. My family and I could have made an impact on our town. Their impact could have changed the nation and I could indeed have changed the world.

UNKNOWN MONK, A.D. 1100

He Wishes for the Cloths of Heaven

BY WILLIAM BUTLER YEATS

Had I the heavens' embroidered cloths,

Enwrought with golden and silver light,

The blue and the dim and the dark cloths

Of night and light and the half-light,

I would spread the cloths under your feet:

But I, being poor, have only my dreams;

I have spread my dreams under your feet;

Tread softly because you tread on my dreams.

JOHN ADAMS TO HIS SON, JOHN QUINCY ADAMS

MARCH 13, 1813

In the letter excerpted here, John Adams writes of observing his granddaughters, Abigail and Susanna, blowing soap bubbles with his pipe.

They fill the air of the room with their bubbles, their air balloons,

which roll and shine reflecting the light of the fire and candles,

and are very beautiful. There can be no more perfect emblem of

the physical and political and theological scenes of human life.

Morality only is eternal. All the rest is balloon and bubble

from the cradle to the grave.

from CROSSING TO SAFETY

BY WALLACE STEGNER

FROM THE HIGH PORCH, the woods pitching down to the lake are more than a known and loved place. They are a habitat we were once fully adapted to, a sort of Peaceable Kingdom where species such as ours might evolve unchallenged and find their step on the staircase of being. Sitting with it all under my eye, I am struck once more, as I was up on the Wightman road, by its changelessness. The light is nostalgic about mornings past and optimistic about mornings to come.

I sit uninterrupted by much beyond birdsong and the occasional knocking and door-slamming of waking noises from the compound cottages hidden in the trees off to the left. Only once is there anything like an intrusion—a motorboat sound that develops and grows until a white boat with a water skier dangling behind it bursts around the point and swerves into the cove, leading a broadening wake across which the skier cuts figures. They embroider a big loop around the cove and roar out again, the noise dropping abruptly as they round the point.

CROSSING TO SAFETY

Early in the morning for such capers. And, I have to admit, a sign of change. In the old days forty academics, angry as disturbed dwarfs, would already have been swarming out of their think houses to demand that the nuisance be abated.

But apart from that one invasion, peace, the kind of quiet I used to know on this porch. I remember the first time we came here, and what we were then, and that brings to mind my age, four years past sixty. Though I have been busy, perhaps overbusy, all my life, it seems to me now that I have accomplished little that matters, that the books have never come up to what was in my head, and that the rewards—the comfortable income, the public notice, the  literary prizes, and the honorary degrees—have been tinsel, not what a grown man should be content with.

What ever happened to the passion we all had to improve ourselves, live up to our potential, leave a mark on the world? Our hottest arguments were always about how we could *contribute*. We

did not care about the rewards. We were young and earnest. We never kidded ourselves that we had the political gifts to reorder society or insure social justice. Beyond a basic minimum, money was not a goal we respected. Some of us suspected that money wasn't even very good for people—hence Charity's leaning toward austerity and the simple life. But we all hoped, in whatever way our capacities permitted, to define and illustrate the worthy life. With me it was always to be done in words; Sid too, though with less confidence. With Sally it was sympathy, human understanding, a tenderness toward human cussedness or frailty. And with Charity it was organization, order, action, assistance to the uncertain, and direction to the wavering.

Leave a mark on the world. Instead, the world has left marks on us. We got older. Life chastened us so that now we lie waiting to die, or walk on canes, or sit on porches where once the young juices flowed strongly, and feel old and inept and confused. In certain moods I might bleat that we were all trapped, though of course we are no more trapped than most people. And all of us, I suppose, could at least be grateful that our lives have not turned out harmful or destructive. We might even look enviable to the less lucky. I give headroom to a sort of chastened indulgence, for foolish and green and optimistic as I myself was, and lamely as I have limped *that* last miles of this marathon, I can't charge myself with real ill will. Nor Sally, nor Sid, nor Charity—any of the foursome. We made plenty of mistakes, but we never tripped anybody to gain an advantage, or took illegal shortcuts when no judge was around. We have all jogged and panted it out the whole way.

I didn't know myself well, and still don't. But I did know, and know now, the few people I loved and trusted. My feeling for them is one part of me I have never quarreled with, even though my relations with them have more than once been abrasive.

In high school, in Albuquerque, New Mexico, a bunch of us spent a whole year reading Cicero—*De Senectute*, on old age; *De Amicitia*, on friendship. *De Senectute*, with all its resigned wisdom, I will probably never be capable of living up to or imitating. But *De Amicitia* I could make a stab at, and could have any time in the last thirty-four years.

Quietness

BY JALAL AL-DIN RUMI

Inside this new love, die.
Your way begins on the other side.
Become the sky.
Take an axe to the prison wall.
Escape.
Walk out like someone suddenly born into color.
Do it now.
You're covered with thick cloud.
Slide out the side. Die,
and be quiet. Quietness is the surest sign
that you've died.
Your old life was a frantic running
from silence.

The speechless full moon
comes out now.

*A friend is a present
you give to yourself.*

ROBERT LOUIS STEVENSON

EVERYBODY WANTS to make some money and I don't blame them.

I want to make some money.

I did make some money.

Now I want to keep it to myself.

It's hard, because people will take your money.

You ever have somebody owe you money and have the nerve to wear new clothes around you? I mean *brand new clothes*, and they're pointing them out like,

Neither A Borrower Nor A Lender Be

BY CHRIS ROCK

"Hey, look at what I done picked up."

"Well, did you see my money while you were there?"

If you lend someone money you have to get it back quickly, otherwise they get *used* to owing you money. It becomes a character trait: you have a fat friend, you have a bald friend, you have a friend who owes you about fifty dollars. This is the friend who has your money for so long that they start telling you about [stuff] they're getting ready to buy.

FRIEND: Next week we going to buy a house.

YOU: I guess you're going to be fifty dollars short, huh?

When people owe you money and they don't repay it quickly, eventually you have to confront them. You have to hunt them down. You've got to turn into Baretta. You've got to walk right up into their face and say, "Didn't I give you that fifty dollars? Wasn't that you? Wasn't that me? Wasn't that my hand? Wasn't that your hand? Yes, I gave you fifty dollars."

After you go through all that, they'll say, "Man, I forgot."

Now you know that's a lie. You *know*. How the *#@!! can you forget where you got some free money from? You don't forget that. If you find $50 on the ground, you're going to remember that for the rest of your life. Every time you walk by that spot, you think, "That's where I found fifty dollars. Right here. April fourteenth, nineteen seventy-two. I remember, I remember. I was a cloudy day, about sixty-eight degrees, and I was wearing my black hat. I loved that hat. And it was about forty-two percent humidity outside and my momma was pregnant with Warren. And I told her, 'Don't drink when you're pregnant.' Now Warren got three toes. Anyway, this is the spot. I looked at the ground and saw ten dimes, four quarters, and a forty-eight-dollar bill."

Dharma

By Billy Collins

The way the dog trots out the front door
every morning
without a hat or an umbrella,
without any money
or the keys to her doghouse
never fails to fill the saucer of my heart
with milky admiration.

Who provides a finer example
of a life without encumbrance—
Thoreau in his curtainless hut
with a single plate, a single spoon?
Gandhi with his staff and his holy diapers?

Off she goes into the material world
with nothing but her brown coat
and her modest blue collar.
following only her wet nose,
the twin portals of her steady breathing,
followed only by the plume of her tail.

If only she did not shove the cat aside
every morning
and eat all his food
what a model of self-containment
    she would be,
what a paragon of earthly detachment.
If only she were not so eager
for a rub behind the ears,
so acrobatic in her welcomes,
if only I were not her god.

KEN BURNS

HAMPSHIRE COLLEGE
MAY 16, 1987

...PHOTOGRAPHY CAME OF AGE with the Civil War, and more than a million images were taken in four years for a public obsessed with seeing, and perhaps also thereby subduing, the shock and carnage they were inflicting on one another. But the public appetite for war photographs, fantastic during the war, dropped off sharply after Appomattox. Mathew Brady went bankrupt. Thousands of photographs were lost, forgotten, mislaid, or misused. Glass plate negatives were often sold to gardeners, not for their images but for the glass itself. In the years immediately following Appomattox, the sun slowly burned the filmy image of war from countless greenhouse gardens across the country, as if the memories might be erased. Still later the glass would be used as lenses in the faceplates of World War I gas masks.

...So it comes down to us, whether we know it, or want to know it, or not. I think we must want to know it, and to know it, we must listen to it and see it, not let the image fade. It is alarming to reflect upon how many of the burning issues that for some reason seemed self-evident twenty years ago have faded from public concern in the last twelve, since I graduated here with my bare feet and my hair down my back. It is not enough to blame it all on the ultimate glass plate negative, TV. We must take more responsibility for our memories than that.

A few weeks ago I was in New Orleans and saw an old friend, a retired judge named Cecil Morgan. Cecil was a fierce opponent of Huey Long's in the Louisiana legislature in the thirties, but that's another story. This time he brought out for me an old book written by his ancestor, James Morris Morgan, who had fought with the Confederates in the Civil War. It was called *Recollections of a Rebel Reefer*—a reference to a midshipman in the Navy, by the way. But what really caught my eye was a letter stuck in the book, a letter to old James Morgan's great-niece Louise. Let me read it to you:

Dear Louise,

When the incidents recorded in this volume seem ancient to you, try to realize that I can remember your grandfather's grandmother Morgan and her tales of how she danced with George Washington.

The past to the aged does not seem as far away as does the dim future, and the only thing that abides with us always is the love of those who are dear to us.

Affectionately,
your old great-uncle,
James Morris Morgan

What I am trying to say in all of this is that there is a profound connection between remembering and freedom and human attachment. That's what history is to me. And forgetting is the opposite of all that: It is a kind of slavery and the worst kind of human detachment. Somewhere in the Statue of Liberty film, a film I made with another Hampshire graduate, Buddy Squires, the writer James Baldwin remarked that no one was ever born who agreed to be a slave. But then, he continued, multitudes and multitudes of people enslave *themselves* every hour of every day to this or that doctrine, this or that delusion of safety, this or that lie: Anti-Semites are slaves to delusion; people who hate Negroes are slaves; people who love money are slaves. We are living in a universe really of willing slaves, Baldwin said, which is what makes the concept of liberty and the concept of freedom so dangerous.

And which is why we must remember, even when, precisely when, what memory has to tell us is appalling. It has seemed to me that the meaning of our freedom as Americans is the freedom of memory, which is also a kind of obligation. We must remember that our country was born under the sign that all men were created equal, but we must remember also that that proclamation did not include blacks or women or the poor. We must remember that Abraham Lincoln signed the Emancipation Proclamation, but we must also remember that Lincoln thought of recolonizing black Americans to Panama or Africa as late as April of 1861 as the guns opened up at Fort Sumpter. We must remember that the Thirteenth and Fourteenth Amendments secured some kind of equality before the law for blacks. But we must also remember that equality as human fact did not come at once, has still to come, and if we do not believe that, *we forget*.

So what do we make of all this? Let me speak directly to the graduating class. As you pursue the future, your future, pursue the past. Let it be your guide. Know the history of your country, not because it is knowledge to accumulate but because it arms you in the best kind of way.

Learn about your family. Find out about your grandmother's grandfather. Where was he in 1861? It will help you, I promise. Read about your history. Read David McCullough's *The Great Bridge*, the best love story around. Read about Sam Houston and his remarkable life. Find out about the real Martin Luther King, not the instant image of him but the student of Gandhi. Read Shelby Foote's stunning history of the Civil War; he is the closest thing we have to Homer. Read Mary Chesnut's Diary, the best diary kept during that period....

There is a cartoon I saw recently which pictures a group of men standing in hell, the flames licking up around them. One man is speaking to the others; he says, "Apparently over two hundred screen credits didn't mean a damn thing." Avoid the word "career" and even "profession." They are concerned with money and position. Continue to investigate.

Have a style, by all means have a style, but remember that fashion itself has a cold center. There is nothing behind it.

Travel. Don't get stuck in one place. I was fortunate this year to see four different springs. In Louisiana, Missouri, Virginia, and now New England. This is your annual chance to learn about the thousand shades of green there are. It is a tonic.

Whatever you do, walk over the Brooklyn Bridge.

You might even visit Appomattox, where the country was reunited. Finally, Shelby Foote once wrote, "This new unity was best defined, perhaps, by the change in number of a simple verb. In common speech, abroad as well as on this side of the ocean, once the nation emerged form the crucible of that war, 'the United States *are*' became 'the United States *is*.'"

Do not neglect your work, but start families. Make babies, lots of them. Say twenty-five. Send them all to Hampshire.

God bless the commonwealth of Massachusetts.

The good old days were never that good, believe me. The good new days are today, and better *days are coming tomorrow. Our greatest songs are still unsung.*

HUBERT H. HUMPHREY

Tomorrow

BY CHARLES STROUSE

The sun'll come out tomorrow
Bet your bottom dollar that tomorrow
There'll be sun!

Jus' thinking about tomorrow
Clears away the cobwebs and the sorrow
Till there's none.

When I'm stuck with a day that's gray and lonely,
I just stick out my chin and grim and say:

Oh! The sun'll come out tomorrow
So you got to hang on till tomorrow
Come what may!

Tomorrow, tomorrow, I love ya tomorrow,
You're always a day away.

Tomorrow, tomorrow, I love ya tomorrow,
You're always a day away.

Things to Think

BY ROBERT BLY

Think in ways you've never thought before
If the phone rings, think of it as carrying a message
Larger than anything you've ever heard,
Vaster than a hundred lines of Yeats.

Think that someone may bring a bear to your door,
Maybe wounded and deranged; or think that a moose
Has risen out of the lake, and he's carrying on his antlers
A child of your own whom you've never seen.

When someone knocks on the door, think that he's about
To give you something large: tell you you're forgiven,
Or that it's not necessary to work all the time, or that it's
Been decided that if you lie down no one will die.

from "THE OCEAN" and "A VISION OF THE WORLD"

JOHN CHEEVER

...I AWOKE AT THREE, feeling terribly sad, and feeling rebelliously that I didn't want to study sadness, madness, melancholy, and despair. I wanted to study triumphs, the rediscoveries of love, all that I know in the world to be decent, radiant, and clear....

And I know that the sound of rain will wake some lovers, and that its sound will seem to be a part of that force that has thrust them into one another's arms. Then I sit up in bed and exclaim aloud to myself, "Valor! Love! Virtue! Compassion! Splendor! Kindness! Wisdom! Beauty!" The words seem to have the colors of the earth, and as I recite them I feel my hopefulness mount until I am contented and at peace with the night.

POET ANNE SEXTON TO
HER 15-YEAR-old DAUGHTER LINDA

APRIL 1969

Wed — 2:45 P.M.

Dear Linda,

I am in the middle of a flight to St. Louis to give a reading. I was reading a NEW YORKER story that made me think of my mother and all alone in the seat I whispered to her "I know, Mother, I know." (Found a pen!) And I thought of you—someday flying somewhere all alone and me dead perhaps and you wishing to speak to me.

And I want to speak back. (Linda, maybe it won't be flying, maybe it will be at your OWN kitchen table drinking tea some afternoon when you are 40. ANYTIME.)—I want to say back.

1st I love you.

2. You never let me down.

3. I know. I was there once. I TOO, was 40 and
   with a dead mother who I needed still.

This is my message to the 40-year-old Linda. No matter what happens you were always my bobolink, my special Linda Gray. Life is

not easy. It is awfully lonely. I know that. Now you too know it—
wherever you are, Linda, talking to me. But I've had a good life—I
wrote unhappy—but I lived to the hilt. You too, Linda—Live to the
HILT! To the top. I love you, 40-year-old Linda, and I love what you
do, what you find, what you are!—Be your own woman. Belong to
those you love. Talk to my poems, and talk to your heart—I'm in
both: if you need me. I lied, Linda. I did love my mother and she loved
me. She never held me but I miss her, so that I have to deny I ever
loved her—or she me! Silly Anne! So there!

XOXOXO
Mom

I Will Survive

WORDS AND MUSIC BY DINO FEKARIS AND FREDDIE PERREN

At first I was afraid, I was petrified;
Kept thinkin' I could never live without you by my side.
But then, I spent so many nights thinkin' how you did me wrong
And I grew strong
And I learned how to get along.
And so you're back from outer space.
I just walk in to find you here with that sad look upon your face.
I should have change that stupid lock.
I should have made you leave your key,
if I'd've known for just one second you'd be back to bother me.

Go on now go, walk out the door;
Just turn around, now, 'cause you're not welcome any more.
Weren't you the one who tried to hurt me with good-bye?
Did you think I'd crumble,
Did you think I'd lay down and die.
Oh no, not I,
I will survive.
Oh as long as I know how to love,
I know I'll stay alive.
I've got all my life to live,
I've got all my love to give and I'll survive,
I will survive!

It took all the strength I had not to fall apart;
Kept tryin' hard to mend the pieces of my broken heart.
And I spent, oh, so many nights just feelin' sorry for myself,
I used to cry,
But now I hold my head up high.
And you see me,
Somebody new,
I'm not that chained up little person still in love with you.
And so you felt like droppin' in and just expect me to be free.
Well now, I'm savin' all my lovin' for someone who's lovin' me.

Go on now go, walk out the door;
Just turn around, now, 'cause you're not welcome any more.
Weren't you the one who tried to hurt me with good-bye?
Did you think I'd crumble,
did you think I'd lay down and die.
Oh no, not I,
I will survive.
Oh as long as I know how to love,
I know I'll stay alive.
I've got all my life to live,
I've got all my love to give and I'll survive,
I will survive!

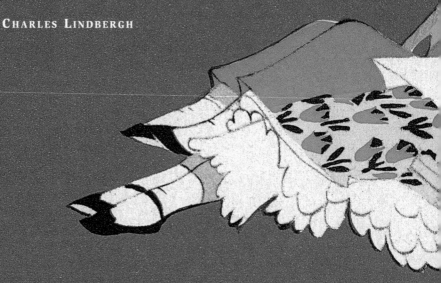

It is the greatest shot of adrenaline to be doing what you've wanted to do so badly. You almost feel like you could fly without the plane.

CHARLES LINDBERGH

Leap Before You Look

BY W. H. AUDEN

The sense of danger must not disappear:
The way is certainly both short and steep,
However gradual it looks from here;
Look if you like, but you will have to leap.

Tough-minded men get mushy in their sleep
And break the by-laws any fool can keep;
It is not the convention but the fear
That has a tendency to disappear.

The worried efforts of the busy heap,
The dirt, the imprecision, and the beer
Produce a few smart wisecracks every year;
Laugh if you can, but you will have to leap.

The clothes that are considered right to wear
Will not be either sensible or cheap,
So long as we consent to live like sheep
And never mention those who disappear.

Much can be said for social savoir-faire,
But to rejoice when no one else is there
Is even harder than it is to weep;
No one is watching, but you have to leap.

A solitude ten thousand fathoms deep
Sustains the bed on which we lie, my dear:
Although I love you, you will have to leap;
Our dream of safety has to disappear.

CREATING BALANCE, HARMONY, AND SUCCESS: FENG SHUI

*If you want to encourage change in your life,
move 27 things in your house.* —Chinese Proverb

A re you drowning in a sea of clutter? Do you keep bumping into the furniture? Are your houseplants sickly? Do your windows need a good washing? Most people live with such imperfections everyday. But taken in combination, these exasperating flaws have the power to wear you down both physically and psychologically. Maybe it's time to get your house in order, literally. Feng Shui can help.

The 3,000-year-old practice of creating harmonious environments, Feng Shui (pronounced Fung Shway) centers on establishing the proper balance of Ch'i—the vital life-source that lives in and supports all things, animate and inanimate.

Traditional Feng Shui stresses balancing elements in your home using the principles of yin and yang and the five elements (Wood, Fire, Earth, Metal, and Water). It also employs what is called a

Bagua Map which helps you place items in "auspicious" locations in your house. But first, here are the three primary principles that govern the ancient Chinese art and philosophy. Their practical applications can be employed by anyone, and they are:

Everything is "alive."

Everything is connected.

Everything is constantly changing.

EVERYTHING IS ALIVE

How can understanding these principles be of any use to you? It's quite practical, really. If you accept that everything in your home contains life forces—your orchid, your pet goldfish, even your stapler—you will surround yourself with things that support your growth and sense of well-being. If 80 percent of the items you own are of no use to you, then it's time to make a change. Things you don't use or like hold negative energy, or Ch'i. They clutter your life, occupying valuable space in your home and mind. The simplest objects—family photographs, a scarf your sister knitted, a toothbrush—have value and therefore contain vital Ch'i. Paring down to the essentials can have a very cleansing effect, and help you to take better care of the things you love.

EVERYTHING IS CONNECTED

Understanding that all things are connected provides you with a holistic perspective. Living in a harmonious space offers peace of mind. A healthy environment has the power to lift your spirits and mind. If your home is a warm, comfortable place where you feel safe, you will certainly enjoy the time you spend there. Conversely, if your home is cluttered and disorganized (and you can never find your keys and wallet before you can leave the house), it can affect your punctuality, and therefore your job security, and therefore your financial standing, and therefore your family's welfare, and therefore your health. This may seem like an exaggerated example, but the simplest things can have a large impact when we are habitually associated with them.

EVERYTHING IS CONSTANTLY CHANGING

It may surprise you to learn that maintaining a harmonious environment doesn't mean that you can "fix" your house once and never change it again. Since you are continually evolving with ever-changing goals, desires, and tastes, your environment should change to support your growth. For example, when you move, your inevitably get rid of things that are no longer useful. Or, when you return from vacation or a business trip, you are inspired to make changes in your home from something you learned while you were away.

If you are interested in delving deeper into the art of Feng Shui, then understanding the principles of the Bagua is essential. The Feng Shui Bagua Map stems from the *I Ching* (*The Book of Changes*) by Lao Tzu. Bagua refers to the eight essential energies or treasures in the universe that govern our lives. When applied to Feng Shui, the Bagua Map can be used to discover which parts of your home correspond to the different areas of your life. On the following page is an example of a Bagua Map:

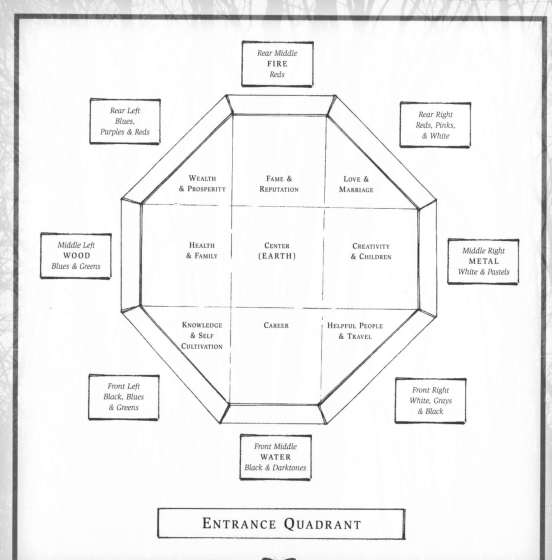

Rear Middle
FIRE
Reds

Rear Left
Blues,
Purples & Reds

Rear Right
Reds, Pinks,
& White

WEALTH
& PROSPERITY

FAME &
REPUTATION

LOVE &
MARRIAGE

Middle Left
WOOD
Blues & Greens

HEALTH
& FAMILY

CENTER
(EARTH)

CREATIVITY
& CHILDREN

Middle Right
METAL
White & Pastels

KNOWLEDGE
& SELF
CULTIVATION

CAREER

HELPFUL PEOPLE
& TRAVEL

Front Left
Black, Blues
& Greens

Front Right
White, Grays
& Black

Front Middle
WATER
Black & Darktones

ENTRANCE QUADRANT

Now, imagine you have a bird's-eye view of your home or apartment. If you were to place a Bagua Map directly over your dwelling—aligning the Entrance Quadrant with your front door—you could see which "corners" correspond to the various treasures.

Using the color and element coding of the Bagua, you can beautify your respective corners, thereby enhancing the overall Ch'i of your space. Colors can be conveyed with the use of paint, art, upholstery, etc. You may also wish to place symbolic objects in each area (e.g., a goldfish in a clean aquarium will enhance your Career corner). Above all else, make sure you love all the objects and colors used for the enhancements. If you use an object or color you don't like just because it matches the criteria for your corner, it will fail to have the desired effect.

So what if your dwelling is not shaped like a square (most spaces aren't), and some of the "corners" on your map extend beyond your exterior walls? For example, the "Children & Creativity" corner of your house may be missing. What do you do? First off, don't panic! If it extends into your yard or patio, you can use that outdoor space as your corner. Simply use white and pastel flowers, and place a whimsical sculpture of children or other representative object in that area. Using outdoor lighting can also anchor a missing corner. If you don't have access or control over the space that would finish off your corner, you can still enhance the energy of that area, or "fix" the flow of Ch'i inside your space. This can be achieved with the use of plants, mirrors, and crystals. Placing a mirror on one or two of the walls will make the indentation seem to disappear. If there are windows on one or two walls, you can hang a round crystal in a window and place a beautiful plant nearby to stimulate and circulate the Ch'i.

Once you've successfully worked with your structure as a whole, you may wish to use the Bagua to map your individual rooms. Don't feel as though you need to deal with every room in order to get it right. Start with the rooms that represent the areas of your life you wish to enhance. Again, use the entrance as your key for orienting the Bagua Map. If there are two doors, use the one that is most frequently used.

FENG SHUI ESSENTIALS:

The kitchen in your home, no matter the location, represents your financial well-being. A clean kitchen is therefore very important: in particular, the stove.

Obtrusive corners, interior columns, or bulky furniture in the center of a room can easily block the flow of Ch'i. This is sometimes hard to avoid in a large, open space. You can fix this problem by dissecting a room visually.

In general, square items hold energy while round items move energy along.

Always keep bathroom doors and the toilet-seat lids closed. This avoids having your luck or money "go down the toilet."

Mirrors can unblock stagnant energy. But be careful that the rest of the room you are placing a mirror in is harmonious. Mirrors can "double" other imbalances.

No one likes to be stared at, and your television can act as an enormous black eye watching your every move. Cover or conceal all televisions either with a cloth or inside a cabinet.

Lighting can enhance the Ch'i of any room. Lights that point up can "fix" a low ceiling. Fluorescent lighting, however, has the reverse effect. It depletes Ch'i with its flicker and its limited light spectrum. Use incandescent or halogen lights whenever possible. Fitting fluorescent fixtures with full-spectrum bulbs can also be helpful—though the problem of flickering light still remains.

It is a good idea to place a wind chime, bells, or a music box in areas such as "Career," "Love," or "Creativity." Pleasing sounds welcome Ch'i and create new opportunities.

Water features also generate pleasing sounds. They can stimulate the Ch'i in any area you wish to enhance.

It stands to reason that people who live in comfortable surroundings live happier, healthier, more productive lives. The time it takes to create your peaceful home is time well spent. Even if your living situation is temporary, that's no excuse! Nurture yourself now.

The Green Stream

WANG WEI

To get to the yellow flower river
I always follow the green water stream
Among the hills there must be a thousand twists
The distance there cannot be fifty miles
There is the murmur of water among rocks
And the quietness of colors deep in pines
Lightly, lightly drifting water-chestnuts
Clearly, clearly mirrored reeds and rushes
I have always been lover of tranquility
And when I see this clear stream so calm
I want to stay on some great rock
And sit forever on and on.

This is your life, not someone else's. It is your own feeling of what is important, not what people will say. Sooner or later, you are bound to discover that you cannot please all of the people around you all of the time. Some of them will attribute to you motives you never dreamed of. Some of them will misinterpret your words and actions, making them completely alien to you. So you had better learn fairly early that you must not expect to have everyone understand what you say and what you do. The important thing is to be sure that those who love you, whether family or friends, understand as nearly as you can make them understand. If they believe in you, they will trust your motives. But do not ask or expect to have anyone with you on everything. Do not try for it. To reach such a state of unanimity would mean that you would risk losing your own individuality to attain it.

ELEANOR ROOSEVELT

ZEN AND THE ART OF MOTORCYCLE MAINTENANCE

By Robert Pirsig

MOUNTAINS SHOULD BE CLIMBED with as little effort as possible and without desire. The reality of your own nature should determine the speed. If you become restless, speed up. If you become winded, slow down. You climb the mountain in an equilibrium between restlessness and exhaustion. Then, when you're no longer thinking ahead, each footstep isn't just a means to an end but a unique event in itself. *This* leaf has jagged edges. *This* rock looks loose. From *this* place the snow is less visible, even though closer. These are things you should notice anyway. To live only for some future goal is shallow. It's the sides of the mountain which sustain life, not the top. Here's where things grow.

But of course, without the top you can't have any sides. It's the top that *defines* the sides. So on we go...we have a long way ... no hurry ... just one step after the next... with a little Chautauqua for entertainment....Mental reflection is so much more interesting than TV it's a shame more people don't switch over to it. They probably think what they hear is unimportant but it never is.

PHOTOGRAPHER ANSEL ADAMS TO HIS FRIEND, CEDRIC WRIGHT

JUNE 10, 1937

Dear Cedric,

A strange thing happened to me today. I saw a big thundercloud move down over Half Dome, and it was so big and clear and brilliant that it made me see many things that were drifting around inside of me; things that related to those who are loved and those who are real friends.

For the first time I KNOW what love is; what friends are; and what art should be.

Love is a seeking for a way of life; the way that cannot be followed alone; the resonance of all spiritual and physical things. Children are not only of flesh and blood—children may be ideas, thoughts, emotions. The person of the one who is loved is a form composed of a myriad mirrors reflecting and illuminating the powers and the thoughts and the emotions that are within you, and flashing another kind of light from within. No words or deeds may encompass it.

Friendship is another form of love—more passive perhaps, but full of the transmitting and acceptance of things like thunderclouds and grass and the clean reality of granite.

Art is both love and friendship, and understanding; the desire to give. It is not charity, which is the giving of Things, it is more than kindness which is the giving of self. It is both the taking and giving of beauty, the turning out to the light the inner folds of the awareness of the spirit. It is the recreation on another plane of the realities of the world; the tragic and wonderful realities of earth and men, and of all the inter-relations of these.

I wish the thundercloud had moved up over Tahoe and let loose on you; I could wish you nothing finer.

Ansel

TONI MORRISON

I WANT TO TALK ABOUT the activity you are always warned against as being wasteful, impractical, hopeless. I want to talk about dreaming.... We are in a mess, you know, and we have to get out....

Well, now, you may be asking yourself, "What is all of this? I can't save the world. What about my life? I didn't come here for this. I didn't even ask to come here. I didn't ask to be born." Didn't you? I put it to you that you did. You not only asked to be born, you insisted on your life. That's why you're here. There's no other reason. It's too easy not to have been born, and now that you're here, you have to do something. Something you respect, don't you? Your parents may have wanted you, but they did not dream you up. You did that. I'm just urging you to continue the dream you started, because dreaming is not irresponsible. It's first order, human business. It's not entertainment, you know. It's work. When Martin Luther King said, "I have a dream," he wasn't playing; he was serious. When he imagined it, envisioned, created it in his own mind, it began. Now we have to dream it too and give it the heft and stretch and longevity it deserves, but don't let anybody convince you this is the way the world is and therefore must be. It must be the way it ought to be....

You are not helpless and you're not heartless, and you have time. Thank you.

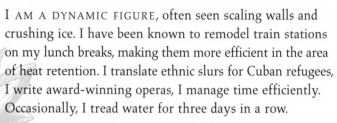

I AM A DYNAMIC FIGURE, often seen scaling walls and crushing ice. I have been known to remodel train stations on my lunch breaks, making them more efficient in the area of heat retention. I translate ethnic slurs for Cuban refugees, I write award-winning operas, I manage time efficiently. Occasionally, I tread water for three days in a row.

But I Have Not Yet Gone to College

HUGH GALLAGHER

I woo women with my sensuous and godlike trombone playing, I can pilot bicycles up severe inclines with un-flagging speed, and I cook Thirty-Minute Brownies in twenty minutes. I am an expert in stucco, a veteran in love, and an outlaw in Peru.

Using only a hoe and a large glass of water, I once single-handedly defended a small village in the Amazon Basin from a horde of ferocious army ants. I play blue-grass cello, I was scouted by the Mets, I am the subject of numerous documentaries. When I'm bored, I build large suspension bridges in my yard. I enjoy urban hang gliding. On Wednesdays, after school, I repair electrical appliances free of charge.

I am an abstract artist, a concrete analyst, and a ruth-less bookie. Critics worldwide swoon over my original line of corduroy evening wear. I don't perspire. I am a private citizen, yet I receive fan mail. I have been caller number nine and have won the weekend passes. Last summer I toured New Jersey with a traveling centrifugal-force demonstration. I bat .400. My deft floral arrangements have earned me fame in international botany circles. Children trust me.

I can hurl tennis rackets at small moving objects with deadly accuracy. I once read *Paradise Lost*, *Moby Dick*, and *David Copperfield* in one day and still had time to refurbish an entire dining room that evening. I know the exact location of every food item in the supermarket. I have performed several covert operations for the CIA. I sleep once a week; when I do sleep, I sleep in a chair. While on vacation in Canada, I successfully negotiated with a group of terrorists who had seized a small bakery. The laws of physics do not apply to me.

I balance, I weave, I dodge, I frolic, and my bills are all paid. On weekends, to let off steam, I participate in full-contact origami. Years ago I discovered the meaning of life but forgot to write it down. I have made extraordinary four course meals using only a mouli and a toaster oven. I breed prize-winning clams. I have won bullfights in San Juan, cliff-diving competitions in Sri Lanka, and spelling bees at the Kremlin. I have played Hamlet, I have performed open-heart surgery, and I have spoken with Elvis.

But I have not yet gone to college.

Forever Young

WORDS AND MUSIC BY BOB DYLAN

May God bless and keep you always
May your wishes all come true
May you always do for others
And let others do for you.

May you build a ladder to the stars
And climb on ev'ry rung
May you stay forever young.
Forever young
Forever young
May you stay forever young.

May you grow up to be righteous
May you grow up to be true
May you always know the truth
And see the lights surrounding you.

May you always be courageous
Stand up right and be strong
May you stay forever young.
Forever young
Forever young
May you stay
Forever young.

May your hands always be busy
May your feet always be swift
May you have a strong foundation
When the winds of changes shift.
May your heart always be joyful
May your song always be sung
May you stay forever young.

PSALM 23:1–7

KING JAMES BIBLE

A PSALM OF DAVID. The LORD is my shepherd;
I shall not want.

He maketh me to lie down in green pastures:
he leadeth me beside the still waters.

He restoreth my soul: he leadeth me in the paths of
righteousness for his name's sake.

Yea, though I walk through the valley of the
shadow of death, I will fear no evil: for thou art with
me; thy rod and thy staff they comfort me.

Thou preparest a table before me in the presence
of mine enemies: thou anointest my head with oil;
my cup runneth over.

Surely goodness and mercy shall follow me all the
days of my life: and I will dwell in the house of the
LORD for ever.

From **Leaves of Grass**

By Walt Whitman

Has any one supposed it lucky to be born?
I hasten to inform him or her it is
    just as lucky to die, and I know it.

I pass death with the dying and birth
    with the new-wash'd babe, and am not
    contain'd between my hat and boots,
And peruse manifold objects,
    no two alike and every one good,
The earth good and the stars good,
    and their adjuncts all good.

I am not an earth nor an adjunct
    of an earth,
I am the mate and companion of people,
    all just as immortaland fathomless
    as myself,
(They do not know how immortal,
    but I know.)

Every kind for itself and its own,
    for me mine male and female,
For me those that have been boys
    and that love women,
For me the man that is proud and feels
    how it stings to be slighted,
For me the sweet-heart and the old maid,
    for me mothers
    and the mothers of mothers,
For me lips that have smiled,
    eyes that have shed tears,
For me children and the begetters
    of children.

COLIN POWELL

FISK UNIVERSITY
MAY 4, 1992

...WHAT WE MUST NEVER LOSE is faith. Faith that in the end right will prevail. Faith in the basic goodness of America and in the basic goodness of Americans.

We must remember that America is a family. There may be differences and disputes in our family but we must not allow the family to be broken into warring factions.

In a few moments you will become members of that family. Here's what I want you to do.

First, I want you to believe in yourself. You have to know that you are capable, that you are competent, that you are good. Your family and Fisk University have seen to that. But *you* have to believe it. I want you to believe that there is nothing—NOTHING—you cannot accomplish by hard work and commitment. Let nothing or no one ever destroy that belief you have in yourself.

Second, I want you to believe in America with all your heart, with all your mind, with all your soul, and with all your body. I've traveled around this world, and I've seen a hundred countries, and I've got to tell you there is no better place or system on earth than that which we enjoy here in America.

America is the hope and promise of the world. We are still, as Abraham Lincoln said, "the last, best hope of earth."

Third, I want you to find strength in your diversity. Let the fact that you are black or yellow or white be a source of pride and inspiration to you. Draw strength from it. Let it be someone else's problem, but never yours. Never hide behind it or use it as an excuse for not doing your best.

We all have to live here together— Asian Americans, African Americans, Hispanic Americans, all of us.

Divided, fighting amongst ourselves, walking separate lines of diversity, we are as weak as newborn babies.

Together, intertwining our many differences and diversities into a mosaic of strength, we will prevail over the darkness of racism. I want you to love one another, I want you to respect one another, see the best in each other. Share each other's pain and joy.

I want you to fight racism. I want you to rail against it. We have to make sure that it bleeds to death in this country once and for all.

As you move forward, I want you to remember those who are still struggling. We must reach back, we must all reach down, we must all work together to pull our people, to pull all Americans out of the violence, out of the dank and soul-damning world of drugs, out of the turmoil of our inner cities. As we climbed on the backs of others, so must we allow our backs to be used for others to go even higher than we have.

Finally, I want you to raise strong families. I want you to create families and raise children who are God-fearing, who are loving, who are clean, and who are determined to do even better than their parents.

As you raise your families, remember the worst kind of poverty is not economic poverty; it is the poverty of *values*. It is the poverty of *caring*. It is the poverty of *love*.

The other evening Alma and I were privileged to be with Maya Angelou. She talked about her upbringing in Stamp, Arkansas. She told us something her grandmother had said to her many years ago. Her grandmother had said, "Girl, when you cross this threshold, you're going to be *raised*."

So raise your children. Treasure them. Love them. They are our future. We cannot let the generation in front of us go to waste.

To look out at you gives me enormous hope. You look so competent, so strong, so young, so committed, so ready to take on the future, difficult times and all.

Looking at you gives me the same feeling of pride that I get when I look at our soldiers, our sailors, our airmen and marines and coast guardsmen. I know when I see them that there is nothing they can't handle, no difficulty they can't overcome, no challenge they don't relish, no mission they can't perform.

Very soon you too will be soldiers. Soldiers in the exciting struggle of life. Soldiers for education. Soldiers for business. Soldiers for science. And, above all, soldiers for a better America.

I believe in this great land that God blessed and called America—because it is full of young men and women like you. Men and women who will keep this nation moving on down the road to glory, its beacon of freedom lighting up all the dark places of the world until there is no darkness left.

We're counting on you! We're counting on you!

Don't go around saying the world owes you a living; the world owes you nothing; it was here first.

MARK TWAIN

GIVING BACK

If you want happiness
for an hour—take a nap.
If you want happiness
for a day—go fishing.
If you want happiness
for a month—get married.
If you want happiness
for a year—inherit a fortune.
If you want happiness
for a lifetime—help someone else.
—Chinese proverb

Most of us spend the first couple decades of our life wondering: who am I? We spend our early, sometimes angst-riddled, years searching for our identity. It is the next question, however, that can plague us until our dying day: What is my purpose in life? This question usually comes on the heels of our discovery that money isn't everything, work outside the home will end, and that we are not the only person in the universe. It is the quest to answer this question—and not necessarily the answer itself—that can strengthen our character and increase our integrity.

Discovering that the effort we exert in life doesn't always have to involve a money-making venture is a great first step. Next, we learn that our talents can be used to better the lives of those in our personal sphere. Some of us stop there— content to "give back" by helping and caring for our friends and family (a noble cause in itself). But what if we extended our notion of giving back to include problems and people beyond our personal sphere?

Albert Einstein, in his book *The Human Side*, calls for a "widening of our circle of compassion to embrace all living creatures and the whole of nature in its beauty." It sounds like heavy stuff, but it doesn't need to be.

Einstein's command can be achieved in large ways (by mentoring, teaching, volunteering, and donating) or small (by being a courteous driver, giving blood, helping a friend in need, and picking up someone else's litter off the street). So, next time you see a stranger who appears to be having a bad day, smile.

Donate time to the local Parks Department. Become a troop leader for your community's chapter of the Girl/Boy Scouts of America. Volunteer at the area Women's Shelter. Operate the local Help Line/Crisis Line. At the very least, vote in every election for which you are eligible. Or give your time or money to the following organizations:

American Civil Liberties Union (ACLU):
www.aclu.org
125 Broad Street, 18th Floor
New York, New York 10004
212-549-2555
212-549-2648 FAX
National organization dedicated to upholding the Bill of Rights.

Big Brothers Big Sisters of America:
www.bbbsa.org
230 North Thirteenth Street
Philadelphia, PA 19107-1538
215-567-7000
215-567-0394 FAX
National organization that pairs adult volunteers with at-risk youth.

Human Rights Watch: www.hrw.org
350 Fifth Avenue
New York, New York, 10118
212-290-4700
212-736-1300 FAX
International organization that seeks to defend human rights worldwide.

Habitat for Humanity International:
www.habitat.org
121 Habitat Street
Americus, GA 31709-3498
800-HABITAT (800-422-4828, ext. 2551 or 2552
229-924-6935
International organization that works to build or rehabilitate houses for families in need.

Meals on Wheels Association of America:
www.projectmeal.org
1414 Prince Street, Suite 302
Alexandria, Virginia 22314
703-548-5558
National organization that provides home-delivered meal services to people in need.

OXFAM
26 West Street
Boston, MA 02111
800-77OXFAM
617-728-2596 FAX
International organization dedicated to fighting hunger through funding long-term development and disaster relief projects in 28 countries throughout Africa, Asia, the Americas, and the Caribbean.

Proliteracy Worldwide: www.proliteracy.org
1320 Jamesville Avenue
Syracuse, NY 13210
800-448-8878 (Catalog orders ONLY)
315-422-9121
315-472-0002 FAX
National organization that works on a local level to provide adult literacy education.

Save the Children: www.savechildren.net
54 Wilton Road
Westport, CT 06881
800-729-1446
203-221-4000
203-221-4077 FAX
Organization that helps children in need in the United States as well as in more than 50 other countries.

Tails a' Waggin' Rescue: www.animalres-cue.in-motion.net
P.O. Box 37
Whitestown, IN 46075
317-769-2543
317-769-4007 FAX
A non-profit animal rescue organization for abandoned, homeless, and abused animals.

Teach for America:
www.teachforamerica.org
National Office
315 West 36th Street
New York, NY 10018
800-832-1230
212-279-2080
212-279-2081 FAX
National organization that places recent college graduates into 2-year teaching assignments in public schools located in low-income areas.

*Three things in human
life are important:
the first is to be kind.
The second is to be kind.
The third is to be kind.*

HENRY JAMES

A Coat

by WILLIAM BUTLER YEATS

I made my song a coat

Covered with embroideries

Out of old mythologies

From heel to throat;

But the fools caught it,

Wore it in the world's eyes

As though they'd wrought it.

Song, let them take it,

For there's more enterprise

In walking naked.

Author Ayn Rand
to her Fan, Joanne Rondeau

May 22, 1948

Dear Ms. Rondeau:

You asked me to explain the meaning of my sentence in
THE FOUNTAINHEAD: "To say 'I love you' one must know
first how to say the 'I.'"

The meaning of that sentence is contained in the whole
of THE FOUNTAINHEAD. And it is stated right in the speech
on page 400 from which you took that sentence. The
meaning of the "I" is an independent, self-sufficient entity
that DOES NOT EXIST for the sake of any other person.

A person who exists only for the sake of his loved one
is not an independent entity, but a spiritual parasite. The
love of a parasite is worth nothing.

The usual (and very vicious) nonsense preached on the subject of love claims that love is self-sacrifice. A man's SELF is his spirit. If one sacrifices his spirit, who or what is left to feel the love? True love is profoundly SELFISH, in the noblest meaning of the word—it is an expression of one's SELF, of one's highest values. When a person is in love, he seeks his own happiness—and NOT his sacrifice to the loved one. And the loved one would be a monster if she wanted or expected sacrifice.

Any person who wants to live FOR others—for one sweetheart or for the whole of mankind—is a selfless nonentity. An independent "I" is a person who exists for his own sake. Such a person does not make any vicious pretense of self-sacrifice and does not demand it from the person he loves. Which is the only way to be in love and the only form of a self-respecting relationship between two people.

269

Blackbird

BY JOHN LENNON AND PAUL MCCARTNEY

Blackbird singing in the dead of night
Take these broken wings and learn to fly;
All your life you were only waiting for this moment to arise.
Blackbird, fly,
Blackbird, fly, into the light of a dark, black night.

Blackbird, fly,
Blackbird, fly,
into the light of a dark, black night.

Blackbird singing in the dead of night
Take these broken wings and learn to fly;
All your life
You were only waiting for this moment to arise,
You were only waiting for this moment to arise

Blackbird singing in the dead of night
Take these sunken eyes and learn to see;
All your life
you were only waiting for this moment to be free.
Blackbird, fly,
Blackbird, fly, into the light of a dark, black night.

Blackbird, fly,
Blackbird, fly,
into the light of a dark, black night.

Blackbird singing in the dead of night
Take these broken wings and learn to fly;
All your life
You were only waiting for this moment to arise,
You were only waiting for this moment to arise.

271

Tomorrow hopes we have learned something from yesterday.

JOHN WAYNE

from **PERSONAL NARRATIVE**

Jonathan Edwards

...I WALKED ABROAD ALONE, in a solitary place in my father's pasture for contemplation. And as I was walking there, and looking upon the sky and clouds, there came into my mind so sweet a sense of the glorious majesty and grace of God, as I know not how to express.—I seemed to see them both in a sweet conjunction; majesty and meekness joined together; it was a sweet and gentle and holy majesty; and also a majestic meekness, a high and great, and holy gentleness.

After this my sense of divine things gradually increased, and became more and more lively, and had more of that inward sweetness. The appearance of every thing was altered; there seemed to be, as it were, a calm, sweet cast, or appearance of divine glory, in almost every thing...in the sun, moon, and stars; in the clouds and blue sky, in the grass, flowers, trees; in the water and all nature....I often used to sit and view the moon for a long time; and in the day, spent much time in viewing the clouds and sky, to behold the sweet glory of God in these things....Before, I used to be uncommonly terrified with thunder, and to be struck with terror when I saw a thunder-storm rising; but now, on the contrary, it rejoiced me. I felt God, if I may so speak, at the first appearance of a thunder-storm; and used to take the opportunity, at such time, to fix myself in order to view the clouds, and see the lightnings play....While thus engaged, it always seemed natural for me to sing, or chant forth meditations; or to speak my thoughts in soliloquies with a singing voice.

Ode 1.9/To Thaliarchus

BY HORACE

See Mount Soracte shining in the snow.
See how the laboring overladen trees
Can scarcely bear their burdens
   any longer.

See how the streams are frozen
   in the cold.
Bring in the wood and light the fire
   and open
The fourth-year vintage wine
   in the Sabine jars.

O Thaliarchus, as for everything else,
Forget tomorrow. Leave it up to the gods.
Once the gods have decided,
   the winds at sea

Will quiet down, and the sea
   will quiet down,
And these cypresses and old
   ash trees will shake
In the storm no longer.
   Take everything as it comes.

Put down in your books
   as profit every new day
That Fortune allows you to have.
   While you're still young,
And while morose old age is far away,

There's love, there are parties,
   there's dancing and there's music,
There are young people out
   in the city squares together
As evening comes on, there are
   whispers of lovers, there's laughter.

We are all in the gutter,
but some of us are
looking at the stars.

— Oscar Wilde

The development of my philosophy came about as follows: My wife, inviting me to sample her very first soufflé, accidentally dropped a spoonful of it on my foot, fracturing several small bones. Doctors were called in, X-rays taken and examined, and I was ordered to bed for a month. During this convalescence, I turned to the works of some of Western society's most formidable thinkers— a stack of books I had laid aside for just such an eventuality. Scorning chronological order, I began with Kierkegaard

My Philosophy

By Woody Allen

and Sartre, then moved quickly to Spinoza, Hume, Kafka, and Camus. I was not bored, as I had feared I might be; rather, I found myself fascinated by the alacrity with which these great minds unflinchingly attacked morality, art, ethics, life, and death. I remembered my reaction to a typically luminous observation of Kierkegaard's: "Such a relation which relates itself to its own self (that is to say, a self) must either have constituted itself or have been constituted by another." The concept brought tears to my eyes. My word, I thought, to be that clever! (I'm a man who has trouble writing two meaningful sentences on "My Day at the Zoo.") True, the passage was totally incomprehensible to me, but what of it as long as Kierkegaard was having fun? Suddenly confident that metaphysics was the work I had always been meant to do, I took up my pen and began at once to jot down the first of my own musings. The work proceeded apace, and in a mere two afternoons—with time out for dozing and trying to get the two little BBs into the eyes of the bear—I had completed the philosophical work that I am hoping will not be uncovered until after my death, or until the year 3000 (whichever comes first), and which I modestly believe will assure me a place of reverence among history's weightiest thinkers. Here is but a small sample of the main body of intellectual treasure that I leave for posterity, or until the cleaning woman comes.

I. Critique of Pure Dread
In formulating any philosophy, the first consideration must always be: What can we know? That is, what can we be sure we know, or sure that we know we knew it, if indeed it is at all knowable. Or have we simply forgotten it and are too embarrassed to say anything? Descartes hinted at the problem when he wrote, "My mind can never know my body, although it has become quite friendly with my legs." By "knowable," incidentally, I do not mean that which can be known by perception of the senses, or that which can be grasped by the mind, but more that which can be said to be Known or to possess a Knownness or Knowability, or at least something you can mention to a friend.

Can we actually "know" the universe? My God, it's hard enough finding your way around in Chinatown.

The point, however, is: Is there anything out there? And why? And must they be so noisy? Finally, there can be no doubt that the one characteristic of "reality" is that it lacks essence. That is not to say it has no essence, but merely lacks it. (The reality I speak of here is the same one Hobbes described, but a little smaller.) Therefore the Cartesian dictum "I think, therefore I am" might better be expressed "Hey, there goes Edna with a saxophone!" So, then, to know a substance or an idea we must doubt it, and thus, doubting it, come to perceive the qualities it possesses in its finite state, which are truly "in the thing itself," or "of the thing itself," or of something or nothing. If this is clear, we can leave epistemology for the moment.

II. Eschatological Dialectics As a Means of Coping with Shingles

We can say that the universe consists of a substance, and this substance we will call "atoms," or else we will call it "monads." Democritus called it atoms. Liebnitz called it monads. Fortunately, the two men never met, or there would have been a very dull argument. These "particles" were set in motion by some cause or underlying principle, or perhaps something fell someplace. The point is that it's too late to do anything about it now, except possibly to eat plenty of raw fish. This, of course, does not explain why the soul is immortal. Nor does it say anything about an afterlife, or about the feeling my uncle Sender has that he is being followed by Albanians. The causal relationship between the first principle (i.e., God, or a strong wind) and any teleological concept of being (Being) is, according to Pascal, "so ludicrous that it's not even funny (Funny)." Schopenhauer called this "will," but his physician diagnosed it as hay fever. In his later years, he became embittered by it, or more likely because of his increasing suspicion that he was not Mozart.

III. The Cosmos on Five Dollars a Day

What, then, is "beautiful"? The merging of harmony with the just, or the merging of harmony with something that just sounds like "the just"? Possibly harmony should have been merged with "the crust" and this is what's been giving us our trouble. Truth, to be sure, is beauty—or "the necessary." That is, what is good or possessing the qualities of "the good" results in "truth." If it doesn't, you can bet the thing is not beautiful, although it may still be waterproof. I am beginning to think I was right in the first place and that everything should be merged with the crust. Oh, well.

Two Parables

A man approaches a palace. Its only entrance is guarded by some fierce Huns who will only let men named Julius enter. The man tries to bribe the guards by offering them a year's supply of choice chicken parts. They neither scorn his offer nor accept it, but merely take his nose and twist it till it looks like a Molly screw. The man says it is imperative that he enter the palace because he is bringing the emperor a change of underwear. When the guards still refuse, the man begins to Charleston. They seem to enjoy his dancing but soon become morose over the treatment of the Navajos by the federal government. Out of breath, the man collapses. He dies, never having seen the emperor and owing the Steinway people sixty dollars on a piano he had rented from them in August.

I am given a message to deliver to a general. I ride and ride, but the general's headquarters seem to get farther and farther away. Finally, a giant black panther leaps upon me and devours my mind and heart. This puts a terrific crimp in my evening. No matter how hard I try, I cannot catch the general, whom I see running in the distance in his shorts and whispering the word "nutmeg" to his enemies.

Aphorisms

It is impossible to experience one's own death objectively and still carry a tune.

The universe is merely a fleeting idea in God's mind—a pretty uncomfortable thought, particularly if you've just made a down payment on a house.

Eternal nothingness is O.K. if you're dressed for it.

If only Dionysus were alive! Where would he eat?

Not only is there no God, but try getting a plumber on weekends.

Somehow I can't believe that there are any heights that can't be scaled by a man who knows the secrets of making dreams come true. This special secret, it seems to me, can be summarized in four C's. They are curiosity, confidence, courage, and constancy, and the greatest of all is confidence. When you believe in a thing, believe in it all the way, implicitly and unquestionably.

WALT DISNEY

Look for the Silver Lining

BY JEROME KERN

Please don't be offended
   if I preach to you a while,
Tears are out of place in eyes
   that were meant to smile.
There's a way to make your
   very biggest troubles small,
Here's the happy secret of it all:

CHORUS
Look for the silver lining
Whene'er a cloud appears in the blue.
Remember somewhere the sun is shining
And so the right thing to do is make it
   shine for you.

A heart full of joy and gladness
Will always banish sadness and strife
So always look for the silver lining
And try to find the sunny side of life.

As I wash my dishes, I'll be following
   your plan,
Till I see the brightness in ev'ry pot and
   pan.
I am sure your point of view will ease
   the daily grind,
So I'll keep repeating in my mind:

(CHORUS)

CARL SAGAN

...WE OWE OUR LIVES—not just the quality of our lives, but the existence of our lives—to technology. Most people on earth would be dead if not for modern agriculture and modern medicine. At the same time, that technology permits weapons of mass destruction, permits inadvertent changes in the environment that sustains us all.

Clearly before us is the very dicey job of using these enormous powers wisely. This is something that we haven't had much experience in because we've never had powers this great. The capability both for good and for evil is unexcelled. And that means that this generation—you young women and men—has an absolute key role to play in the long adventure of the human species.

Because of the newness of co-education...I want to share a few thoughts with you....We are very close relatives of the chimpanzees. We share 99.6 percent of active genes with chimpanzees, which means there's a lot about us we can learn from chimps. Now it's clear that chimp society is— how shall I say?—testosterone ridden. By no means all, but a great deal of the aggression and intimidation is something the males feel especially comfortable and happy with.

In times of stress and crowding there's something very interesting that happens. This is brought out, for example, in the Arnhem colony of chimps in the Netherlands. The males, when they get annoyed, use rocks and stones. They like to throw things. The females are not into missiles. In times of crisis the males can be seen gathering lots of stones—their arms full, their fists clenched—to carry over and throw at their adversaries. The females walk over to these stone-laden males and pry their fingers open, take the stones out, and deposit them on the ground....

I have a feeling that the hereditary predisposition for females as mediators and peacemakers is in the 99.6 percent of the genes we share with the chimps. And that leads me to wonder what the world would be like if women played a role proportionate to their numbers. I don't mean just the occasional woman prime minister who beats the boys at their own game. I mean real, proportionate sharing of power. I mean half, not a few percent, of the members of the Senate—women. I mean half, not zero, of the succession of Presidents being women. I mean half the Joint Chiefs of Staff as women. I mean half of the chief executive officers of major corporations as women.

Maybe it would change nothing. Maybe under these circumstances, the institutions predetermine human behavior, and it doesn't matter whether you're male or female; if you're chairman of the Joint Chiefs of Staff, you have an attitude, and it doesn't matter what brought you to it.

But I like to think that's not the case, that in a world in which women truly share power...we would have a more just, more humane, and more hopeful future. Maybe this is just a pipe dream. But it's a kind of fantasy I couldn't help but have in thinking about this class.

You've been given, in your four years here, some of the tools to preserve and, where necessary, to change the society and the global civilization. No one says this is easy. There are enormous forces of inertia and resistance to any change at all. And there are those who benefit and prosper from there being no change. Nevertheless, it's clear that our civilization is in trouble, that significant changes are necessary. And I hope you will make them.

One of the most important tools is skeptical or critical thinking. Put another way, equip yourself with a baloney detection kit. Because there is an enormous amount of baloney that has to be winnowed out before the few shining gems of truth can be glimpsed. And a lot of that baloney is proffered by those in power. That's their job. Part of the job of education is to be able to tell what's baloney and what's not.

The urgency you feel to make changes is just the extent that change will be made. Don't sit this one out. Don't play it safe. Understand the world, and change it where it needs to be changed. Where it doesn't, leave it alone. Make our society better. Make a world worthy of the children that your generation will bear.

In spite of everything, yes, let's!

VINCENT VAN GOGH

you shall above all things
be glad and young

BY E. E. CUMMINGS

you shall above all things be glad and young.
For if you're young,whatever life you wear

it will become you;and if you are glad
whatever's living will yourself become.
Girlboys may nothing more than boygirls need:
i can entirely her only love

whose any mystery makes every man's
flesh put space on;and his mind take off time

that you should ever think,may god forbid
and(in his mercy)your true lover spare:
for that way knowledge lies,the foetal grave
called progress,and negation's dead undoom.

I'd rather learn from one bird how to sing
than teach ten thousand stars how not to dance

MERENGUE, MASSAGE, AND MANGO SORBET:
THE ART OF SENSUALITY

"Kama is the enjoyment of appropriate objects by the five senses of hearing, feeling, seeing, tasting and smelling, assisted by the mind together with the soul." —from The Kama Sutra (Aphorisms of Love)

Picture yourself on the beach at sunset. What do you notice? A gentle breeze caresses your face. Cool sand nestles between your toes. Salt air penetrates your nostrils. Rhythmic waves resound in your ears. Striations of lilac and indigo clouds surrounding a blood-orange sun hit your gaze. A warmth flows through you as your partner reaches for your hand. Is this the stuff of a romance novel? Well, maybe it seems a bit "Hollywood" on paper, but it still must strike a cord. You've known moments like this one. Wouldn't it be marvelous to have more of them?

This somewhat cliché beach scenario is filled with sensory delights. But what do you do if the place where you live is landlocked? You can't be running across the country all the time for your sensuality fix. Well, your ability to get the best out of life is intimately tied to your sensory acumen. It is entirely possible to fine-tune your senses and achieve greater awareness of the wonder around you.

Start off by making a list of your favorite things (e.g., chocolate, mango sorbet, foot massages, going to the ballet, outdoor showers, "date night" with your sweetie, playing soccer, the smell in the air after a hard rain, dancing, walking in the woods, art museums, long baths, a vase full of peonies, etc.). Think about what each of your favorites does to your senses. When you soak in the tub, for example, what does it do for your senses? It warms your skin—the largest organ of the body, and therefore the one with the greatest sensory potential. It makes you feel light, and relaxes your muscles. Well, what if you turned it up a notch and transformed your bathroom into a spa? How does a sparkling clean tub of cozy water with bergamot oil sound? Add some candles, your favorite music, a bath pillow, a glass of champagne! Now you've turned the experience into a party for the senses!

You can have greater enjoyment of life simply by paying attention to your experiences and surroundings. The next time you find yourself at an art museum, find a painting or sculpture you are drawn to and really study it. Look at it from far away and up close. Examine the materials and techniques used to create it. Internalize how it makes you feel. Next time you are watching television with your significant other, instead of sitting in close proximity to each other, cuddle. Or, better yet, turn the TV off and give each other a massage. Really feel the warmth of your partner's hands on your skin. Allow yourself to feel the safety and security of your intimacy. Next time you're making dinner, don't just cook—cook with spices! Don't just look at flowers—smell and touch them. Don't just hear music—experience it with your emotions. Trade your flannel pajamas in for some silk ones, or nothing at all. Go skinny-dipping. Look into the eyes of someone you love while they speak—you'll hear better that way! You can truly turn each day into an adventure for the senses.

THE WORLD ACCORDING TO GARP

BY JOHN IRVING

GARP WATCHED WALT, and this calmed him. Garp relished having such close scrutiny of the child; he lay beside Walt and smelled the boy's fresh breath, remembering when Duncan's breath had turned sour in his sleep in that grownup's way. It had been an unpleasant sensation for Garp, shortly after Duncan turned six, to smell that Duncan's breath was stale and faintly foul in his sleep. It was as if the process of decay, of slowly dying, was already begun in him. This was Garp's first awareness of the mortality of his son. There appeared with this odor the first discolorations and stains on Duncan's perfect teeth. Perhaps it was just that Duncan was Garp's firstborn child, but Garp worried more about Duncan than he worried about Walt—even though a five-year-old seems more prone (than a ten-year-old) to the usual childhood accidents. And what are *they*? Garp wondered. Being hit by cars? Choking to death on peanuts? Being stolen by strangers? Cancer, for example, was a stranger.

There was so much to worry about, when worrying about children, and Garp worried so much about everything; at times, especially in these throes of insomnia, Garp thought himself to be psychologically unfit for parenthood. Then he worried about *that*, too, and felt all the more anxious for his children. What if their most dangerous enemy turned out to be *him*?

Author Jack London to His 14-year-old Daughter, Joan

September 16, 1915

Dear Joan:

…Joan, you are on the right track. Never hesitate at making yourself a dainty, delightful girl and woman. There is a girl's pride and a woman's pride in this, and it is indeed a fine pride. On the one hand, of course, never over-dress. On the other hand, never be a frump. No matter how wonderful are the thoughts that burn in your brain, always, physically, and in dress, make yourself a delight to all eyes that behold you.

I have met a number of philosophers. They were real philosophers. Their minds were wonderful minds. But they did not take baths, and they did not change their socks and it almost turned one's stomach to sit at table with them.

Our bodies are as glorious as our minds, and, just as one cannot maintain a high mind in a filthy body, by the same token one cannot keep a high mind and high pride when said body is not dressed beautifully, delightfully, charmingly. Nothing would your Daddy ask better of you in this world than that you have a high mind, a high pride, a find body, and, just as all the rest, a beautifully dressed body.

I do not think you will lose your head. I think, as I read this last letter of yours, that I understand that you have balance, and a woman's balance at that. Never forget the noble things of the spirit, on the other hand, never let your body be ignoble, never let the garmenture of your body be ignoble. As regards the garmenture of your body, learn to do much with little, never to over-do, and to keep such a balance between your garmenture and your mind that both garmenture and mind are beautiful.

I shall not say anything to you about your method of saving, about Bess's method of saving, but there is much I should like to say to you, and, in the meantime I think a lot about it. You are on the right track. Go ahead. Develop your mind to its utmost beauty; and keep your body in pace with your mind.

Daddy

Love After Love

by DEREK WALCOTT

The time will come
When, with elation,
You will greet yourself arriving
At your own door, in your own mirror,
And each will smile at the other's welcome,

And say, sit here, Eat.
You will love again the stranger who was your self.
Give wine. Give bread. Give back your heart
To itself, to the stranger who has loved you

All your life, whom you ignored
For another, who knows you by heart.
Take down the love letters from the bookshelf,

The photographs, the desperate notes,
Peel your image from the mirror.
Sit. Feast on your life.

There are only two ways to live your life. One is as though nothing is a miracle. The other is as though everything is a miracle.

ALBERT EINSTEIN

306

I RECENTLY TURNED FIFTY, which is young for a tree, mid-life for an elephant, and ancient for a quarter-miler, whose son now says, "Dad, I just can't run the quarter with you anymore unless I bring something to read."

Fifty is a nice number for the states in the Union or for a national speed limit, but it is not a number that I was prepared to have hung on *me*. Fifty is supposed to be my *father's* age, but now Bill Cosby, *Junior*, is stuck with these elevated digits and everything they mean. A few days ago, a friend tried to cheer me up by saying, "Fifty is what forty used to be." He had made an inspirational point; and while I ponder it, my forty-year-old knees are suggesting I sit down and my forty-year-old eyes are looking for their glasses, whose location has been forgotten by my forty-year-old mind.

Where To, Old Cos?

BY BILL COSBY

Am I over the hill? They keep telling me that the hill has been moved, that people are younger than ever. And I keep telling *them* that the high-jump bar has dropped from the six feet five I once easily cleared to the four feet nothing that is a Berlin wall for me now. It is not a pretty sight to see a man jumping a tennis net and going down like something snagged by a lobster fisherman.

"You're not getting older, you're getting better," says Dr. Joyce Brothers. This, however, is the kind of doctor who inspires a second opinion.

And so, as I approach the day when my tennis court jumping will be over the balls (or maybe the lines), I am moved to share some thoughts on aging with you, in case you happen to be getting older too. I am moved to reveal how aging feels to me—physically, mentally, and emotionally. Getting older, of course, is a distinctly better change than the one that brings you eulogies. In fact, a poet named Robert Browning considered it the best change of all:

Grow old along with me!
The best is yet to be.

On the days when I need aspirin to get out of bed, Browning is clearly a minor poet; but he was an optimist and there is always comfort in his lines, no matter how much you ache.

Whether or not Browning was right, most of my first fifty years have been golden ones. I have been an exceedingly lucky man, so I will settle for what is ahead being as good as what has gone by. I find myself moving toward what is ahead with a curious blend of both fighting and accepting the aging of Cosby, hoping that the philosopher was right when he said, "Old is always fifteen years from now."

Turning fifty has not bothered me, but people keep saying it *should* have, for fifty is one of those milestone ages that end in zero. Of course, in America *every* age ending in zero is considered a milestone age. Fifty is called the Big Five-O, but Forty is The Big Four-O and Thirty is The Big Three-O. A few months ago, my youngest daughter hit the Big One-O and she wasn't happy about it.

"I wish there were more single figures," she said.

Although reaching this half-century mark has not traumatized me, it *has* left me with disbelief about the flight of time. It seems that only yesterday I was fifteen and old people were people of forty, who were always going someplace to sit down. And now *I* am doing the sitting; and now my wife is telling me, "You *sit* too much. You should get up and *do* something."

"Okay," I say, "let's have some sex."

"Just *sit* there."

When I was eight, an uncle said, "Bill, how long would you like to live?"

"A hundred million years," I replied.

"That's a ripe old age. I wonder what you'll *look* like at a hundred million."

"Oh, I'll just be me," I said.

Now, however, considerably short of the hundred-million mark, I am having to learn to accept a new me, one who has to drink skim milk, which looks like the wash for a paintbrush; one whose stomach refuses to process another jalapeño pepper; and one for whom a lobster is crustacean cyanide.

"If you want a lobster," my doctor says, "just eat the shell."

Have I *also* become just the shell? Well, in one or two places, the meat *is* missing. For example, I am now a man with the ability to dial a telephone number and, while the phone is ringing, forget whom he is calling. Just yesterday, I made such a blind call and a person answered with a voice I did not know. Like a burglar doing research, I quickly hung up, and then I thought about age.

Wiser men than I have thought about age and have never figured out anything to do except say, "Happy birthday." What, after all, *is* old? To a child of seven, ten is old; and to a child of ten, twenty-five is middle-aged and fifty is an archaeological exhibit. And to me, a man of seventy is...what I want to be, weighing 195, playing tennis with convalescents, and hearing well enough to hear one of my grandchildren sweetly say, "Grandpa, was 'The Cosby Show' anything like 'I Love Lucy'?"

THE MOTH AND THE STAR

By James Thurber

A YOUNG AND IMPRESSIONABLE moth once set his heart on a certain star. He told his mother about this and she counseled him to set his heart on a bridge lamp instead. "Stars aren't the thing to hang around," she said; "lamps are the thing to hang around." "You get somewhere that way," said the moth's father. "You don't get anywhere chasing stars." But the moth would not heed the words of either parent. Every evening at dusk when the star came out he would start flying toward it and every morning at dawn he would crawl back home worn out with his vain endeavor. One day his father said to him, "You haven't burned a wing in months, boy, and it looks to me as if you were never going to. All your brothers have been badly burned flying around street lamps and all your sisters have been terribly singed flying around house

lamps. Come on, now, get out of here and get yourself scorched! A big strapping moth like you without a mark on him!"

The moth left his father's house, but he would not fly around street lamps and he would not fly around house lamps. He went right on trying to reach the star, which was four and one-third light years, or twenty-five trillion miles, away. The moth thought it was just caught in the top branches of an elm. He never did reach the star, but he went right on trying, night after night, and when he was a very, very old moth he began to think that he really had reached the star and he went around saying so. This gave him a deep and lasting pleasure, and he lived to a great old age. His parents and his brothers and his sisters had all been burned to death when they were quite young.

Moral: *Who flies afar from the sphere of our sorrow is here today and here tomorrow.*

Everyone has it within his
power to say, this I am today,
that I shall be tomorrow.

Louis L'Amour

The Glory of Love

BY BILLY HILL

You've got to give a little, take a little
And let your poor heart break a little,
That's the story of,
That's the glory of love,

You've got to laugh a little, cry a little
Before the clouds roll by a little
That's the story of,
That's the glory of love.

As long as there's the two of us
We've got the world and all its charms
And when the world is through with us
We've got each other's arms
You've got to win a little, lose a little
And always have the blues a little
That's the story of,
That's the glory of love.

*To laugh often and much, to win the respect of
intelligent people and the affection of children;
to earn the appreciation of honest critics and endure
the betrayal of false friends; to appreciate beauty;
to find the best in others; to leave the world a
bit better, whether by a healthy child, a garden
patch or a redeemed social condition; to know
even one life has breathed easier because
you have lived. This is to have succeeded.*

RALPH WALDO EMERSON

MADELEINE ALBRIGHT

MOUNT HOLYOKE COLLEGE
MAY 25, 1997

…AS INDIVIDUALS EACH OF US MUST CHOOSE whether to live our lives narrowly, selfishly, and complacently or to act with courage and faith.

As a nation America must choose whether to turn inward and betray the lessons of history or to seize the opportunity before us to shape history.…

The Berlin Wall is now a memory. We could be satisfied with that. Instead we are enlarging and adapting NATO and striving to create a future for Europe in which every democracy—including Russia—is our partner and every partner is a builder of peace.

Largely because of U.S. leadership, nuclear weapons no longer target our homes. We could relax. Instead we are working to reduce nuclear arsenals further, eliminate chemical weapons, end the child-maiming scourge of land mines, and ratify a treaty that would ban nuclear explosions forever.…

We have built a growing world economy in which those with modern skills and available capital have done very well. We could stop there. Instead we are pursuing a broader prosperity, in which those entrapped by poverty and discrimination are empowered to share and in which every democracy on every continent will be included.

In our lifetimes we have seen enormous advances in the status of women. We could now lower our

voices and—as some suggest—sit sedately down. Instead women everywhere—whether bumping against a glass ceiling or rising from a dirt floor—are standing up, spreading the word that we are ready to claim our rightful place as full citizens and full participants in every society on earth.

Mount Holyoke is the home, to borrow Wendy Wasserstein's phrase, of "uncommon women." But we know that there are uncommon women in all corners of the globe.

In recent years I have met in Sarajevo with women weighted down by personal grief reaching out across ethnic lines to rebuild their shattered society.

In Burundi I have seen women taking the lead in efforts to avoid the fate of neighboring Rwanda, where violence left three quarters of the population female, and one half of the women widows.

In Guatemala I have talked to women striving to ensure that their new peace endures and is accompanied by justice and an end to discrimination and abuse.

And in Burma I have met with a remarkable woman named Aung San Suu Kyi, who risks her life every day to keep alive the hope for democracy in her country.

These women have in common a determination to chart their own path and, by so doing, to alter for the better the course of their country or community.

Each has suffered blows, but each has proceeded with courage. Each has persevered.

As you go along your own road in life, you will, if you aim high enough, also meet resistance, for as Robert Kennedy once said, "If there's nobody in your way, it's because you're not going anywhere." But no matter how tough the opposition may seem, have courage still—and persevere.

There is no doubt, if you aim high your efforts to change the world or improve the lot of those around you do not mean much in the grand scheme of things But no matter how impotent you may sometimes feel, have courage still—and persevere.

It is certain, if you aim high enough, that you will find your strongest beliefs ridiculed and challenged; principles that you cherish may be derisively dismissed by those claiming to be more practical or realistic than you. But no matter how weary you may become in persuading others to see the value in what you value, have courage still—and persevere.

Inevitably, if you aim high enough, you will be buffeted by demands of family, friends, and employment that will conspire to distract you from your course. But no matter how difficult it may be to meet the commitments you have made, have courage still—and persevere.

It has been said that all work that is worth anything is done in faith.

This morning, in these beautiful surroundings, at this celebration of warm memory and high expectation, I summon you in the name of this historic college and of all who have passed through its halls, to embrace the faith that your courage and your perseverance will make a difference and that every life enriched by your giving, every friend touched by your affection, every soul inspired by your passion, and every barrier to justice brought down by your determination will ennoble your own life, inspire others, serve your country, and explode outward the boundaries of what is achievable on this earth.

From **CAT'S CRADLE**

By Kurt Vonnegut

"HE WAS SUPPOSED TO BE our commencement speaker,"
said Sandra.

"Who was?" I asked.

"Dr. Hoenikker—the old man."

"What did he say?"

"He didn't show up."

"So you didn't get a commencement address?"

"Oh, we got one. Dr. Breed, the one you're gonna see tomorrow,
he showed up, all out of breath, and he gave some kind of talk."

"What did he say?"

"He said he hoped a lot of us would have careers in science," she said.
She didn't see anything funny in that. She was remembering a lesson that
had impressed her. She was repeating it gropingly, dutifully. "He said, the
trouble with the world was . . ."

She had to stop and think.

"The trouble with the world was," she continued hesitatingly, "that
people were still superstitious instead of scientific. He said if everybody
would study science more, there wouldn't be all the trouble there was."

"He said science was going to discover the basic secret of life someday," the bartender put in. He scratched his head and frowned. "Didn't I read in the paper the other day where they'd finally found out what it was?"

"I missed that," I murmured.

"I saw that," said Sandra. "About two days ago."

"That's right," said the bartender.

"What *is* the secret of life?" I asked.

"I forget," said Sandra.

"Protein," the bartender declared. "They found out something about protein."

"Yeah," said Sandra, "that's it."

To me, if life boils down to one significant thing, it's movement. To live is to keep moving. Unfortunately, this means that for the rest of our lives we're going to be looking for boxes.

When you're moving, your whole world is boxes. That's all you think about. "Boxes, where are there boxes?" You just wander down the street going in and out of stores, "Are there boxes here? Have you seen any boxes?" It's all you think about. You can't even talk to people, you can't concentrate. "Will you shut up? I'm looking for boxes!"

Homestretch

BY JERRY SEINFELD

After a while, you become like a bloodhound on the scent. You walk into a store, "There's boxes here. Don't tell me you don't have boxes, dammit, I can smell 'em!" I become obsessed. "I love the smell of cardboard in the morning." You could be at a funeral, everyone's mourning, crying around you, you're looking at the casket. "That's a nice box. Does anybody know where that guy got that box? When he's done with it, you think I could get that? It's got some nice handles on it. My stereo would fit right in there."

I mean that's what death is, really, it's the last big move of your life. The hearse is like the van, the pallbearers are your close friends, the only ones you could really ask to help you with a big move like that. And the casket is that great, perfect box you've been looking for your whole life. The only problem is once you find it, you're in it.

Ode To My Socks

BY PABLO NERUDA

Maru Mori brought me
a pair
of socks
which she knitted with her
own
sheepherder hands,
two socks as soft
as rabbits.
I slipped my feet
into them
as if they were
two
cases
knitted
with threads of
twilight
and the pelt of sheep.

Outrageous socks,
my feet became
two fish
made of wool,
two long sharks
of ultramarine blue
crossed
by one golden hair,
two gigantic blackbirds,
two cannons:
my feet
were honored in this way
by
these
heavenly
socks.
They were
so beautiful
that for the first time
my feet seemed to me
unacceptable
like two decrepit
firemen, firemen
unworthy

of that embroidered
fire,
of those luminous
socks.

Nevertheless,
I resisted
the sharp temptation
to save them
as schoolboys
keep fireflies,
as scholars
collect
sacred documents,
I resisted
the wild impulse
to put them
in a golden
cage
and each day give them
birdseed
and chunks of pink melon.
Like explorers
in the jungle

who hand over the rare
green deer
to the roasting spit
and eat it
with remorse,
I stretched out
my feet
and pulled on
the
magnificent
socks
and
then my shoes.

And the moral of my ode
it this:
beauty is twice
beauty
and what is good is doubly
good
when it's a matter of two
woolen socks
in winter.

If you fall, boy, you don't have to wallow. Ain't nobody going to think you somebody unless you think so yourself. Don't listen to their talk, boy, they don't have a pot to pee in or a window to throw it out. For God's sake, Jesse, promise me you'll be somebody. Ain't no such thing as "cain't," "cain't" got drowned in a soda bottle. Don't let the Joneses get you down. Nothing is impossible for those who love the Lord. Come hell or high water, if you got guts, boy, ain't nothing nobody can turn you around.

MATILDA BURNS,
JESSE JACKSON'S GRANDMOTHER

Father and Son

WORDS AND MUSIC BY CAT STEVENS

I was once like you are now
And I know that it's not easy
To be calm when you've found
Something going on.
But take your time, think a lot.
I think of everything you've got.
For you will still be here tomorrow
But your dreams may not.

(Chorus)
It's not time to make a change
Just relax, take it easy.
You're still young, that's your fault
There's so much you have to know.
Find a girl, settle down.
If you want you can marry.
Look at me,
I am old but I'm happy

How can I try to explain?
When I do he turns away again.
It's always been the same, same old
story.
From the moment I could talk
I was ordered to listen
Now there's a way and I know
That I have to go away,
I know I have to go.

(Chorus)

All the times that I've cried
Keepin' all the things I knew inside.
It's hard, but it's harder
To ignore it.
If they were right I'd agree
But it's them they know, not me.
Now there's a way and I know
That I have to go away.
I know I have to go.

Nothing Gold Can Stay

by ROBERT FROST

Nature's first green is gold,

Her hardest hue to hold.

Her early leaf's a flower;

But only so an hour.

Then leaf subsides to leaf.

So Eden sank to grief,

So dawn goes down to day.

Nothing gold can stay.

Light tomorrow with today.

ELIZABETH BARRETT BROWNING

341

KEEPING A DREAM JOURNAL

Dreams are the touchstones of our character. —Henry David Thoreau

WHAT ARE DREAMS?

We humans have been eternally fascinated by our dreams. The ancient Greeks believed they were visionary stories relayed by the gods. It wasn't until the 5th century B.C.E. that Plato challenged the concept of the prophetic dream. He understood dreams as nothing other than the inner workings of the dreamer's mind. The Bible revived the notion of supernaturally influenced dreams—the most famous of which was given to Jacob, who dreamed of a ladder stretching from Earth into heaven.

Modern dream theories tend to agree with Plato. Carl Jung (1875–1961), a pupil of Sigmund Freud (1856–1939), saw dreams as the vehicle through which the unconscious mind speaks to the conscious mind. He believed that only through careful study of and reflection on our own dreams might we gain a sense of contentment and completeness.

"The images of the unconscious place a great responsibility upon a man. Failure to understand them...deprives him of his wholeness and imposes a painful fragmentariness on his life."

WHY DO YOU DREAM?

During the course of an average day, you spend 16–18 hours taking in external stimuli. Your brain continually receives more information than you can readily assimilate into your consciousness. That's where dreams come in. When you sleep, your mind is still hard at work—it sorts through all the images and ideas you were unable to consciously act upon throughout the day, and adds to them unresolved issues from the past. The ideas that are floating around in your subconscious mind find their way into your dreams. Since the logic of the unconscious mind is often mysterious, the images you are shown in your dreams rarely have a basis in reality. More frequently, these images are symbols that you must attempt to interpret according to your own unique experience. No one else can assign meaning to the symbols of your dreams. Your dreams are about you, and therefore you are the one person supremely qualified to interpret them.

WHAT ARE YOUR DREAMS TRYING TO TELL YOU?

What secrets do you think your unconscious mind is trying to tell you? Is the key to unlocking your happiness hidden in your dreams? One way to tap into your subconscious is by keeping a dream journal. Successful integration of your conscious and subconscious mind is hard work, but it is work that can provide you with the tools necessary to become a happier, more whole person. The powerful process of keeping a journal will allow you to see inside yourself more clearly than you ever have. Here's how to start the dialog with your subconscious:

Before you write a word, it's a good idea to practice dream recall. Approach this as a skill. Before you go to sleep, tell yourself that you will remember your dreams. Don't get discouraged if it doesn't happen right away. It may take a week or so to establish the habit, and even then you may not recall your dreams every day. If you have trouble, try to read books about dreams before bed. Meditate or pray about dreaming. Research dream symbols.

Once you've established the habit of recalling your dreams, it is time to start recording. Your journal can be anything from a notepad to a handmade book.

Each night before bed, review the previous few dreams you recorded in your journal. Next, write the date on a new page, and write a sentence or two about your day—exciting events, goals you are working toward at home or at work, things that may have upset you, etc. This will help achieve the right frame of mind for linking your conscious and subconscious. As you have been doing with the recall practice, tell yourself you want to remember your dreams and engage with your subconscious.

Keep your journal and pen by your bedside (with a flashlight if you wish). If you wake in the night with a dream memory, jot it down.

When you wake up in the morning, whatever you do, DON'T GET OUT OF BED! First, write anything you remember about your dreams in your journal. Even if you don't remember your whole dream, write down what you do remember. Sometimes key words or images are all that you need to help interpret your dream. You may find it helpful to write out what comes to you with codes and shorthand. An example of a code may be placing a small question mark next to a fuzzy detail that you intend to fill in later. Once you have the broad picture down on paper, you can go back and fill in the details as they come to you. Bits and pieces may be all you recall at first. Your dreams should become more and more lucid with time.

Look over your entry and think about what events may have triggered that particular dream. Write down any connections or interpretations of symbols that come to you.

Carry your journal with you, or a smaller notepad, so you can write down anything you remember during the course of the day. Also, be sure to record when and where the memory came to your attention. This may help you figure out what triggered the memory and evaluate whether or not it plays a role in the dream interpretation.

After several weeks of establishing this habit, you may discover that you are having an easier time recalling your dreams, and that they are more lucid. You may even be an active participant in your dreams. There are ways to encourage more lucid dreaming. Try to remember what you were doing over the past few hours. If you are dreaming, you won't be able to, or it will be illogical, even to your subconscious. Or, you can try to jump up and fly within your dream. Try breathing into your hand or moving or manipulating something with your mind. These tricks generally help you to be able to participate in your dreams and to better remember them in the morning.

You may notice recurring dreams or symbols in your dreams. Pay close attention to these dreams as they are usually an indication that your subconscious is desperately trying to tell you something.

What you do with all the information you compile is up to you. But close observation of the patterns and symbols of your dreams can help you to deal with your fears, inhibitions, insecurities, and other problems. The more you engage with your dreams and act upon what they are trying to tell you, the more self-aware and fulfilled you will be.

Sweet dreams!

Hold Fast Your Dreams

Louise Driscoll

Hold fast your dreams!
Within your heart
Keep one still, secret spot
Where dreams may go,
And, sheltered so,
May thrive and grow
Where doubt and fear are
not.
Oh keep a place apart,
Within your heart,
For little dreams to go!

Think still of lovely things
that are not true.
Let wish and magic work at
will in you.
Be sometimes blind to
sorrow. Make believe!
Forget the calm that lies
In disillusioned eyes.
Though we all know that we
must die,
Yet you and I
May walk like gods and be
Even now at home in
immortality.

We see so many ugly things—
Deceits and wrongs and
quarrelings;
We know, Alas! we know
How quickly fade
The color in the west,
The bloom upon the flower,
The bloom upon the breast
And youth's blind hour.
Yet keep within your heart
A place apart
Where little dreams may go,
May thrive and grow.
Hold fast—hold fast your
dreams!

CORINTHIANS 13: 6-13

NEW TESTAMENT, KING JAMES BIBLE

REJOICETH NOT IN INIQUITY, but rejoiceth in the truth;

Beareth all things, believeth all things, hopeth all things, endureth all things.

Charity never falleth: but whether *there be* prophecies, they shall fail: whether *there be* tongues, they shall cease; whether *there be* knowledge, it shall vanish away.

For we know in part, and we prophesy in part.

But when that which is perfect is come, then that which is in part shall be done away.

When I was a child, I spake as a child, I understood as a child, I thought as a child: but when I became a man, I put away childish things.

For now we see through a glass, darkly; but then face to face: now I know in part; but then shall I know even as also I am known.

And now abideth faith, hope, charity, these three; but the greatest of these *is* charity.

*There will come a time when
you believe everything is finished.
That will be the beginning.*

Louis L'Amour

350